# A Question of Balance

# A Question of Balance

H.R.H. The Duke
of Edinburgh

Michael Russell

First published in Great Britain 1982
by Michael Russell (Publishing) Ltd
The Chantry, Wilton, Salisbury, Wiltshire

Designed by Humphrey Stone

Photoset in 11/14 Ehrhardt
by Santype International Ltd
Salisbury, Wilts
and printed in Great Britain
by Biddles Ltd, Guildford, Surrey



ISBN 0 85955 087 7

# Contents

# Introduction

I make no claim to being a philosopher but every now and then I am invited to address a general, rather than a specialist, audience on any subject of my choosing. In many ways this is a relief from the constraints of having to compose something about the arts, or engineering, or recreation, but it is also rather more of an intellectual challenge. All the arguments have to be dredged up from personal experience and study, and this forces me to reflect and to order my thoughts.

It is not that I ever consciously set out to observe what was going on; it is simply that I found I had absorbed a multitude of impressions, which seemed to come to the surface when I was unwise enough to agree to give a lecture which did not commit me to a particular subject. On a number of those lectures which might be described as having a philosophical tinge to them (and particularly the 1980 St. George's House Lecture), I sought the advice of the Dean of Windsor, the Right Reverend Michael Mann. Out of this collaboration the idea developed of adapting a selection of material into book form; and it is the Dean, I should here gratefully acknowledge, who has borne the editorial brunt of the adaptation.

Every philosophical discussion presents arguments for and against, which have to be weighed. This is particularly so in a period when people seem only too ready to take their point of view to extremes. I believe that most people, having carefully considered all the factors, prefer to adopt a more moderate approach, and it is for this reason that I have called this selection of material *A Question of Balance*.

Though I chose each subject and wrote about it for a particular occasion, I think a common theme does thread its way through the contents of this book. I notice that I keep coming back to the importance and the central position of the individual and the crucial part that human nature plays in every aspect of communal life. If there is any rational explanation for this I suspect it is that I happen to find myself in rather an individual position. I am involved in the activities of a great many groups but the sheer number of these groups makes it impossible to belong completely to any one of them. Furthermore in many cases my involvement is as an active or titular head and that in itself tends both to isolation and objectivity.

Whether it is also partly due to what I learned about Christianity as I grew up or whether I learned more about Christianity from the discovery of individualism I really could not say. However, I am quite certain that the two are linked together and, from what I see going on in the world around me, I am very much inclined to believe that religious conviction is the strongest and probably the only factor in sustaining the dignity and integrity of the individual.

# 1
# Conflict

# Conflict

In the early seventies when Robin Woods, later to become Bishop of Worcester, was Dean of Windsor, he revitalised St. George's and among other things he created a discussion centre out of two very large and no longer needed canon's houses. The purpose was to give people in positions of responsibility and the leaders of thought and opinion an opportunity to discuss contemporary issues with members of the clergy, and to allow the clergy to become better informed about lay opinion. By 1977 a good many people had experience of St. George's House meetings and quite a large informal body of supporters had come into existence. It was the idea of Dean Michael Mann to give these supporters a chance to come together by instituting an annual lecture to be given in St. George's Chapel. Mr. Kingman Brewster, a distinguished academic and university administrator, and at the time the U.S. Ambassador in London, gave the first lecture, 'The Entitlement Society', in 1978. The second was given by M. Paul Marc Henri who spoke about 'Changing Standards in Society'. On both occasions I had taken the chair, so it came as rather a nasty shock when the Dean suggested that I should give the third lecture.*

After many false starts, I decided to look at another element in human conflict. For hundreds of years the relations between nations have been dictated by such things as the

* Windsor Castle, 11 April 1980: 'One Aspect of Human Conflict'.

personalities and ambitions of their leaders, commercial rivalry, and other, mainly incidental, clashes of interest. Now, in the twentieth century, a completely new element has entered the scene. International relations are now dominated by a clash of political ideologies. My intention therefore has been to analyse the causes and consequences of this latest danger to the peace and safety of ordinary people; and to assess the influence of Marxist philosophy on the general relationship of the individual to the State.

There is a classic, if depressing, law that bad news always drives out good news and the worse the news the more space it takes up. As a consequence incidents and events tend to be given much more coverage than the issues themselves. There is a danger, I know, of getting what we call disasters out of proportion simply because they are going on in our lifetime, yet somehow the impression persists that what is going on today is different in some way from previous experience. It seems to me that in recent years man's inhumanity to man has developed a wholly new and a different quality. There seems to have been a remarkable sameness about so much of the violence. The language of justification, the techniques of intimidation and terrorism, the source of weapons and, perhaps most obvious of all, the political structure and style adopted by successful revolutionaries and liberation armies; they all appear to have a quite remarkable family likeness.

This disturbing similarity may be due once again to modern communications which so easily spread the philosophy and language of conflict and revolution from one part of the world to another; and revolutionaries tend to be just as conformist as any other group. There may well be other reasons, but it is surely a curious coincidence that sooner or later, with only a few exceptions, it becomes apparent that at the heart of the terrorist campaign, or of the liberation army, or of the revolutionary movement, or of civil unrest, there is a hard core of Marxists. Furthermore it cannot be entirely coincidence that wherever such a state of conflict exists the terrorists, liberators or revolutionaries are almost invariably supported by money, arms or men and women from countries under Marxist regimes. It therefore seems difficult to avoid the conclusion that the family likeness in so much of modern conflict is, in fact, the likeness of Marx, though, to be fair, it is very doubtful that Marx himself would have been proud of everything that has been perpetrated in his name. But this is a factor he has to share with all political and religious leaders. Certainly there are distinctions to be drawn between Marxism, Communism, Socialism, Leninism, Trotskyism, Stalinism and probably several other 'isms', but I think it is generally accepted that they are all either related to or derived from Marx's analysis and ideology. In much the same way Christianity covers a multitude of variants of the Christian faith.

There are of course plenty of famous philosophers in the history of the world; men who have given us a better understanding of ourselves, of our natures, and of our curious situation in this universe. Some of them became great religious leaders whose influence on morality and on attitudes and beliefs was strong enough to transform men's behaviour and to change their social and political existence. Although their individual teaching varies considerably in detail, in general terms they were agreed about the virtues of love, peace, tolerance and brotherhood and the most successful of them still number their followers in hundreds of millions. Even if Marx never thought of himself as a founder of a religion, the fact remains that his achievement in terms of the numbers of his followers – the number of people who have been attracted by his ideas and the impact he has made on the pattern of human existence – is certainly on the same scale.

The salient points of Marx's life are worth mentioning. He was born in Trier in the Rhineland in 1818, descended on his father's side from a family of eminent rabbis. His father was a prosperous lawyer in the Prussian service who chose to become a Lutheran in 1824; his mother was of Hungarian origin and strangely enough never learned to speak or to read German. Marx himself studied at the Universities of Bonn and Berlin, which in the conditions of the time implies a degree of family affluence. Initially he took up law but soon drifted into philosophy and joined what might be described as the mainstream of militant European socialism, dominated at that time by the materialism of Feuerbach and the dialectic of Hegel. This led to political journalism and agitation and consequently to the necessity for fairly frequent moves from one country to another. In London in 1847 he joined the League of Communists, for whom he and his friend Engels composed *The Communist Manifesto*. (Engels, incidentally, was the son of a German cotton manufacturer with factories in England.) He then spent the last thirty-four years of his life with his aristocratic wife, Jenny von Westphalen, and their family in Soho, almost entirely dependent on whatever support Engels was able to provide. His literary output was considerable but most of his later years were occupied in completing the manuscript of his *Das Kapital*, which he considered to be his main work. Only the first volume was published in his lifetime, the other two volumes were brought out by Engels after his death.

There is nothing very extraordinary about this story. The general pattern of his life was not untypical of any number of middle-class intellectuals and he exhibited many of their characteristics. He appears to have had an enormous capacity for painstaking work, a vivid and forceful literary style, considerable imagination, and a single-minded devotion to a particular philosophy. His weakness, if that is that appropriate word for it, seems to have been a hopelessly unrealistic understanding of human nature. His obsession with science and scientific socialism, with materialism and dialectics, and with academic research, seems to have blinded him to the power, variety and irrational nature of human emotions and talents and to the fact that such qualities of human nature are equally distributed among all people regardless of class or intellect.

Compare Karl Marx's life story with that of Jesus Christ. Disregarding for a moment the divine element, I think it would be fair to say that Jesus was born apparently out of wedlock to a temporarily homeless artisan. He narrowly escaped political murder as a baby and was brought up as a carpenter who spent his life preaching love and forgiveness. Eventually this man of peace was arrested, tortured and tried in secret – against Jewish law – for preaching that God is love. He was condemned to a criminal's death. Perhaps most astonishing of all is that He left nothing in writing. In modern terms He might be described as an underprivileged, colonial, working-class victim of political and religious persecution. Yet He only sought to influence men in their behaviour towards each other through their belief in God and promised paradise in the next world, whereas the middle-class intellectual sought absolute political power and expected to achieve paradise in this world.

It is a further irony that the man who institutionalised class-warfare and glorified totalitarianism should have lived out his life in the safety of a tolerant and peaceful and democratic society, while the man who worked so hard to heal divisions and reconcile enemies should have met such a violent end in what was virtually a theocratic state.

One of the major difficulties about trying to assess Marx's ideas is that they seem to be composed of two separate and distinct elements. One is a scholarly and extensively researched analysis of economic and social history which resulted in the development of the theory of historical materialism. The other is the promotion of a subjective ideology based on the conviction that one vaguely defined group of people was responsible for all the world's social and economic problems. Unfortunately both elements are woven into his works in such a way that it is very difficult to unravel them into their distinctive parts.

The trouble is that no matter how honestly, zealously or objectively people may seek it, it is only to be expected that they will arrive at different estimates of the truth, depending on their analysis of the evidence they choose to use, on their deductive powers and on their judgement. Marx, like many before and since his time, went to considerable lengths to make his selection of facts fit his particular theories. After all, if every one of us were capable of grasping the whole truth about particular aspects of human existence as easily as we can grasp the difference between male and female, or that two plus two equals four, there would be no discussion about such things as politics and religion, and economic analysts would always be right. It is also important to bear in mind that Marx, like any other political writer, was inevitably influenced by the ideas of his predecessors and by the social, economic and industrial attitudes and the conditions of his time, as well as by the intellectual fashions of his contemporaries. This is particularly important because while the basic elements of human nature have remained much the same, social and economic conditions are constantly changing and evolving.

To begin with, it is worth remembering that the French Revolution and the beginning of the Industrial Revolution had taken place only a relatively short time before he was born. The one had shown that an apparently stable and entrenched regime could be overthrown by violence. The other was to demonstrate that pre-industrial society in Europe was coming to an end. Secondly, by the time Marx was learning and observing, the Industrial Revolution in Britain was quite well advanced and, as with all revolutions, its progress was marked by all kinds of excesses, unexpected developments, including a population explosion, and wholly new situations with which the existing forms of social and political organisation were virtually unable to cope. The consequence was to accentuate the differences between the wealthy and the poor, the powerful and the helpless and the controllers and controlled.

However, you cannot very well have something like half the rural population moving into the cities and expect housing, sanitation, schools, hospitals and all the other social infrastructure to appear overnight. The wonder is that so much appeared as quickly as it did. Nor can you give the enterprising people new opportunities to make their fortunes and the more ordinary people the chance to earn comparatively high wages, and expect them to consider with much care all the implications of their eagerness to grasp them. It seems to be one of the unfortunate rules of human nature that whenever people get on to a good thing, they promptly overdo it. Selfishness and thoughtlessness are more to blame than malice.

Equally, you cannot have new industrial enterprises with previously unheard of methods of manufacture springing up like mushrooms and expect Parliament to enact appropriate legislation for their control at the same speed. Even Marx acknowledges that the situation in Britain would have been much worse but for the efforts of reformers in Parliament and the findings of Commissions of Inquiry into the worst scandals and excesses. It is therefore extremely unlikely that conditions at the middle stages of any revolution are any certain guide to what things will be like when the revolution has run its course. This is particularly true of the Industrial Revolution which brought about more radical changes to human life-style than any previous period in history. Yet Marx picked on the nastiest features of industrial life in the middle of this revolution and based on them a general theory for all human behaviour, past, present and future.

One of the consequences of the general process of economic and social evolution, which included the break-up of the feudal system, the enclosure of common land and the Industrial Revolution, was the large increase in the number of wage labourers employed either by landlords or by factory owners. Marx believed very strongly that it was impossible to have a satisfactory society where there was such a crude division between those who owned property and capital and those who had nothing but their wages. Naturally in a purely static situation this would be intolerable, but no human system is static and the freer the system the more quickly the self-correcting mechanism works and the greater the movement between classes is likely to be. Furthermore while it is quite true that the difference between those two groups was very great in Marx's time, the fact is that they occupied the extreme ends of a very wide social spectrum with any number of economic groups in between and it so happens that subsequent evolutionary changes in non-Marxist countries have narrowed this gap very considerably.

Marx lived through the middle of the Industrial Revolution and many of his judgements were made on the basis of the contemporary situation in England. But he was also particularly influenced by Darwin and by the general intellectual atmosphere of his time. Theism had given way to legalism which in turn had given way to liberalism, anti-clericalism, rationalism and utilitarianism. There was a utopian belief that every human problem could be solved by scientific analysis and the operation of altruistic human will. All that was necessary was to identify and eradicate the cause of the problem and everything would immediately become all sweetness and light. Marx was convinced that he had achieved all this in his theory of historical materialism.

Perhaps the most concise statement of this theory is contained in the Preface to *The Communist Manifesto* written by Engels some years after its first publication. Engels put it like this:

> The Manifesto being our joint production, I consider myself bound to state that the fundamental proposition which forms its nucleus belongs to Marx. That proposition is: that in every historical epoch the prevailing mode of economic production and exchange, and the social organisation necessarily following from it, form the basis upon which is built up, and from which alone can be explained, the political and intellectual history of that epoch: that consequently the whole history of mankind (since the dissolution of primitive tribal society, holding land in common ownership) has been a history of class struggles, contests between exploiting and exploited, ruling and oppressed classes; that the history of these class struggles forms a series of evolutions in which, nowadays, a stage has been

> reached where the exploited and oppressed class – the proletariat – cannot attain its emancipation from the sway of the ruling class – the bourgeoisie – without at the same time, and once and for all, emancipating society at large from all exploitation, oppression, class distinctions and class struggles.

I do not think that anyone would seriously quibble with the idea that the modes of production and exchange have a significant influence on political and intellectual attitudes – although in these days the opposite would seem to be nearer the case – but it is stretching a point to suggest that they are the only influence on these attitudes. For one thing it implies that none of the world's great religions has had the slightest influence on individual behaviour or on political and intellectual attitudes at any time or in any society, which seems hardly realistic. Yet this is precisely the message of historical materialism. Man's behaviour is said to be influenced exclusively by class interests and material factors and nothing else. It postulates that man has no spiritual life and consequently that all religion, and hence morality, is completely irrelevant. Therefore exactly how there can be such a thing as a dialogue between Christians and Marxists, as some would suggest, I find very difficult to understand. While it is true that both recognise the need to help the poor and the oppressed, they are certainly not the first or the only people to have had such compassionate ideas.

Lord Hailsham has written: 'The history of politics can be crystallised into a protracted war between freedom and authority.' However, it seems to be a massive oversimplification to suggest that the war between freedom and authority is no more than a series of struggles between classes except, of course, that the more intelligent usually find themselves in positions of authority. Further to suggest that the proletarian revolution against the bourgeoisie will, once and for all, emancipate society at large from all exploitation, oppression, class distinctions and class struggles is patently absurd. The evidence of fifty years of a Marxist-derived regime in the U.S.S.R. seems to be sufficient in itself to disprove such a claim.

One of the features of Marxist analysis is the constant use of group denominations and particularly the references to the bourgeoisie and the proletariat, as if there was no such thing as individual will and conscience. Indeed Marx explains his position in the Preface to *Das Kapital*:

> But here individuals are dealt with only in so far as they are the personifications of economic categories, embodiments of particular class relations and class interests. My standpoint, from which the evolution of the economic formation of society is viewed as a process of natural history, can less than any other make the individual responsible for relations whose creature he socially remains, however much he may subjectively raise himself above them.

In other words human society is like an antheap: every attitude and reaction is ordained by your particular class or occupation. How very different from the teaching of most religions, and particularly from the Christian emphasis on the personal relationship between God and each individual, and thus the primary responsibility of the individual for his moral standards and intellectual attitudes. What sort of an argument is it to say that because all my colleagues and contemporaries are behaving in a certain way, that is the way historical materialism has ordained that I must behave?

Marx even went so far as to suggest that ideas were subject to the same law. 'What else', he wrote, 'does the history of ideas prove than that intellectual production changes its character in proportion as material production is changed?' Are we to infer from this that the steam-engine was responsible for the Victorian novels or that automation gave rise to the permissive society? And what may we expect from the chip?

Marx then goes on to say that 'the ruling ideas of each age have ever been the ideas of its ruling class', which may be true of a dictatorship but is not necessarily true of a democracy with a free press. For example, the ruling ideas in Marxist states reflect only too accurately the qualities of their ruling classes; but this is surely more to do with their ideology than with the character of material production, which hardly varies very much anyway between Marxist and non-Marxist industrial communities.

It is quite a different matter to argue that certain classes and groups share the same interest or are subject to the same temptations. That does not mean that each member has to react to such circumstances in the same way. I think the Christian view would be that no matter what the pressures or temptations in any occupation or situation, each individual must react according to his own conscience in the knowledge that he is directly answerable for it to God. And this, it seems to me, is borne out in practice where the highest and the lowest moral standards can be found in roughly the same proportions at each level of society.

It seems to follow therefore that in the Christian view it is the individual members of a class or group who give it its character and not the other way round. The picture painted by Marx of human life as nothing but a series of lumbering manoeuvres by huge agglomerations of people reacting in unison to particular stimuli, even if it is partially true, is an immensely depressing one. The exercise of individual will and responsibility may be difficult under certain circumstances, and many people may prefer to avoid it as much as possible, but that does not mean that individuality cannot exist at all or, worse still, that it should not be allowed to exist.

One of the most important factors affecting intellectual attitudes in Marx's time was the cult of science, brought on by the steadily increasing number of spectacular discoveries emerging from scientific research and especially by Darwin's theory of natural selection which brought natural history out of myth into science. With all the enthusiasm of those who think they understand it all, some of the intelligentsia lost no time in transferring the application of discoveries in the science of matter to social and behavioural problems. To Marx it seemed obvious that as a man's body was made up of identifiable chemicals, that it responded to electric currents and had other mechanical features, then it must follow that human nature was equally explicable in such materialist terms. Any idea of a divine spark, or an immortal soul, or that an individual had any special value or unique quality was sheer romantic nonsense. The classic flaw in the whole idea surely was that scientific answers only apply to the specific scientific questions. It merely causes confusion if you apply selected scientific answers to social issues.

But Marx went even further: he taught that all human qualities were products of the brain and that the function of the brain was to store experiences, particularly experiences of babyhood and childhood. He believed consequently that environment could change human nature and all that was needed to create perfected personalities was a group of men with the necessary knowledge to seize power and implement the requisite programmes – an idea which has been the essence of totalitarian philosophy since Plato's guardians.

It is curious how many philosophers from Plato to Keynes's time have believed in and advocated the control of society by 'philosopher kings'. According to Plato, 'its kings must be those who have shown the greatest ability in philosophy', but – realistically – he added, 'and the greatest aptitude for war'. Such people may exist in the imagination and occasionally someone with the necessary qualities may briefly dominate the stage of history, but it is a naive appreciation of human nature to imagine that such processed paragons can be invested with the necessary powers and not be tempted to take advantage of their situation. It was precisely to guard against such dangers that the authors of the American Constitution incorporated their 'checks and balances'.

Marx also claimed that his theory made it possible to predict the future. In fact, the present situation (even in Marxist states) bears little relation to any of his predictions. The self-destructive mechanism of capitalism has also failed to materialise. Or perhaps, to be more accurate, capitalism has proved to be a great deal more flexible and adaptable than he ever imagined.

I doubt, for instance, whether anyone could have foreseen that the private capitalism in Britain of Marx's time would have been replaced, to a very large extent, by joint stock companies and by social capitalism in the form of share holding by insurance companies, pension funds and unit trusts.

But while Marx's generalised theory of historical materialism may help us to understand certain aspects of history, it seems to me that one of its greatest weaknesses is that it ignores the purely voluntary and altruistic elements in human nature which are encouraged to flourish in any civilised human society. The concepts of charity (in the voluntary sense), or of obligation, or of a social conscience, hardly exist in Marxist doctrine but there are vast numbers of people of all classes in this country who give money generously to charities and who give their leisure time and energies to voluntary organisations of all kinds and who respond with astonishing speed to the needs of the victims of natural and man-made disasters all over the world. This cannot be swept aside as a sort of fringe phenomenon peculiar to the bourgeoisie and unworthy of consideration by serious political and economic commentators. It is a vitally important factor in life and the very best example of individual initiative and sense of responsibility. It is perhaps because all these things are functions of the human spirit that Marx was unable to recognise them.

The other side of Marx's work was his development of a political ideology which he derived from his analysis of economic and social history. The most significant feature of his ideology appears to be that as a result of the Industrial Revolution the middle class, the bourgeoisie, had become the ruling class and that its exploitation of the proletariat, or working class, by capitalist modes of production was the cause of all the world's economic and social problems. The bourgeoisie had therefore to be destroyed by the abolition of all private property, by the 'abolition of the right of inheritance' and by a 'heavy progressive or graduated income tax'. Plato had much the same idea but he only wanted to deprive the guardians of private property.

As Marx's ideas entailed the confiscation from private capitalists of all means of production, distribution, transport and communication, all these things would have to be centralised in the hands of the State, by which he meant in the hands 'of the proletariat organised as the ruling class'. As he admits in the *Manifesto*:

> In the beginning this cannot be effected except by means of despotic inroads on the rights of property and on the conditions of bourgeois production.

It is no use arguing, he says, that such measures would do away with freedom and individuality because

> The abolition of this state of things is called by the bourgeois abolition of individuality and freedom. And rightly so. The abolition of bourgeois individuality, bourgeois independence, and bourgeois freedom is what is undoubtedly aimed at.

How these things are to be distinguished from proletarian individuality, proletarian independence, and proletarian freedom when the proletariat becomes the ruling class is not exactly clear.

While Marx intended all these measures to destroy the bourgeoisie, he apparently failed to notice that his system would create a bigger and even more powerful ruling class than ever before. The centralisation of all the means of production, distribution and communication in the hands of the State inevitably requires the State to employ a very large number of what are generally known as bureaucrats, which in any reasonable analysis would be classed as bourgeoisie. Perversely enough it was the emergence of this vast new ruling class in the U.S.S.R. which became one of the many bones of contention between Trotsky and Stalin. Trotsky maintained that the workers had been enslaved by Stalin's massive bureaucracy, at the same time hotly denying that he and Lenin had been largely responsible for creating it, or even recognising that such a bureaucracy was an inevitable consequence of Marxist ideology. The supreme irony is that this massive bureaucracy is probably the best guarantee against any change in the system. We have known since Aristotle's time that 'all men are persuaded by considerations of their interest and their interest lies in the maintenance of the established order'.

This was not the only unexpected consequence of Marxist ideology. The idea of taking away property from other people has much more appeal if you have none of your own, but one of the products of confiscatory taxation is the rapid and extensive development of what we call 'fringe benefits', as they are always 'tied' to particular jobs in the same way as the old agricultural 'tied cottage'. The beneficiaries feel that they have gained something but they seem to be unaware that they are in danger of becoming virtual slaves of their employers or of the State. After all, slaves live entirely on 'fringe benefits'.

It is a peculiar irony that the *Manifesto* ordains that 'the first step in the revolution by the working class is to raise the proletariat to the position of the ruling class, to establish democracy'. In practice it was the introduction of universal adult suffrage in the Western democracies that gave the working class real political power, and the introduction of revolutionary Marxism which consolidated the effective power of the new middle-class bureaucrats. Furthermore democracy is a product of a free society; it cannot exist where one class has a monopoly of power.

Of all Marx's ideas the most explosive was his choice of one particular class or group of citizens within a society – distinguished only by their relative wealth and occupations – to be held responsible for everything that is unsatisfactory in that society. He becomes quite vitriolic about the industrial middle class and returns to the attack again and again.

Indeed in some passages of the *Manifesto* he appears to be positively nostalgic for his idea of the pre-bourgeois society. He writes:

> The bourgeoisie, wherever it has got the upper hand, has put an end to all feudal, patriarchal, idyllic relations. It has pitilessly torn asunder the motley feudal ties that bound man to his 'natural superiors', and has left no other bond between man and man than naked self-interest, than callous 'cash payment'.

Not everyone would choose the word 'idyllic' to describe relations in the feudal system; nor, apparently, did it occur to Marx that if you do away with all private property, then literally every single citizen becomes dependent on 'callous cash payment' for his living and is forced into 'naked self-interest' to acquire it.

He goes on:

> It has drowned the most heavenly ecstasies of religious fervour, of chivalrous enthusiasm, of philistine sentimentalism, in the icy water of egotistical calculation . . . In one word, for exploitation, veiled by religious and political illusions, it has substituted naked shameless, direct, brutal exploitation.
>
> The bourgeoisie has stripped of its halo every occupation hitherto honoured and looked up to with reverent awe . . .
>
> The bourgeoisie has torn away from the family its sentimental veil, it has reduced the family relation to a mere money relation.

Our Lord had some strong things to say about the Pharisees and the Sadducees, but He never accused them of anything much more serious than hypocrisy and He never actually suggested that they should be exterminated. The impression that I get from all this is that in a laudable effort to remove the antagonisms which inevitably arise in all societies through the normal operation of human nature and the consequent clashes of interest, Marx has used this theory of historical materialism to make class warfare between the bourgeoisie and the proletariat into what seems to have become a permanent and institutionalised feature of all human existence. His whole theory has become a grand justification for social conflict.

It is true that he saw the class war and revolution as a passing phase:

> In place of the old bourgeois society, with its classes and class antagonism, we shall have an association in which the free development of each is the condition of the free development of all.

However, experience in every known Marxist-based society shows only too clearly that this was a monumental piece of wishful thinking. In Marxist societies the warfare between the traditional bourgeois and the traditional proletariat may be over, but a whole new set of antagonisms have been introduced. There are bitter doctrinal differences and the hatred for the vastly inflated bureaucracy is just as violent and even more frustrated than it may ever have been for the bourgeoisie. The 'despotic inroads' of the secret police and the concentration camps have seen to it that 'free development' has a pretty restricted meaning. Under Stalin the bureaucracy turned on the peasants, the very people the system was supposed to liberate, and treated them with the utmost brutality.

As Professor Kolakowski, author of *The Mainstreams of Marxism*, puts it:

> Marxism is a doctrine of blind confidence that a paradise of universal satisfaction is just around the corner. Almost all the prophecies of Marx and his followers have already proved to be false, but this does not disturb the spiritual certainty of the faithful. . . . In this sense Marxism performs the functions of a religion. . . . But it is a caricature and bogus form of religion since it presents its temporal eschatology as a scientific system which religious mythologies do not purport to be.

While Marxist societies are suffering from one set of consequences of this bogus religion, the societies which have not succumbed to the Marxist revolution have acquired yet another cause of civil strife. On top of the ordinary and passing clashes of interest they have to cope with an ideology of hatred which cannot be eradicated either by success or failure. If the Marxist revolution succeeds, one set of antagonisms is merely replaced by another, even more bitter than before. If, on the other hand, the revolution is prevented, all the spurious justifications for class hatred and class warfare remain to fester and to poison the system. Perhaps one of Marx's worst miscalculations was to forget that if you threaten people with death or the expropriation of their property they are unlikely to give you their loyal support.

One has to admit that Marx had the welfare of the least privileged section of society at heart. Unfortunately his arrogant conviction that his theory comprehended all human problems, his aggressive style, his predilection for totalitarian solutions and dictatorship and his advocacy of State control have had results which not even he could have foreseen. Indeed it seems that he has given the old proverb about the 'road to hell . . .' ample justification. It did not take long, for example, for unscrupulous politicians, who are always on the lookout for means of acquiring power, to realise that a one-party State whose government was in control of all the means of production, distribution, transport and communication was the answer to their prayers. It was only necessary to use Marxist methods to gain control, which means by force if the ballot box will not produce the results, and they were in clover virtually for life. This security of tenure is of course due to the fact that in order to manage all its responsibilities the State needs a very large number of employees, usually well over half the population. Self-interest being what it is, it is obvious that the bureaucracy will see to it that the system is not allowed to be changed. In any case, given the sanctions of the Marxist ideology, it is not very difficult for the leadership to suppress and eliminate any opposition.

There are now a number of such states in existence around the world and it seems to me that they prove two things:

First, that Marxism has given ambitious politicians an absolutely ideal method of acquiring and keeping absolute power. It is a very neat illustration of the truth of Aristotle's comment that 'the end of democracy is freedom . . . of tyranny, the protection of the tyrant'. That this system is not universally popular with the remainder of its citizens seems to be proved by the fact that dissidents are persecuted and that more than one Marxist government has had to take severe measures to prevent its citizens leaving the country. In some cases they have had to build physical obstructions which, unlike Hadrian's Wall or the Great Wall of China, for the first time in history are designed to keep their citizens in, rather than foreigners out.

Second, that as a practical economic system, in the sense of creating material prosperity for the citizens, Marxism has failed in comparison with what Marx described as capitalism but which I think would be more accurately described as the market system. Like democracy the market system is a product of a free society and consequently it allows for risks and experiments in modes of living and politics as well as in technology, and reaps the benefits denied to the Marxist system. Whatever the internal social conditions may be like in a Marxist state, if that state does not have massive natural resources, it is more than likely to be bankrupt and consequently dependent on borrowing from abroad or on external aid. All the evidence from people who have visited and tried to do business in such states is that the system as a whole, to put it kindly, is less than efficient, more than likely to be corrupt and largely incapable of meeting the demand for consumer goods. Yet at the same time massive resources are allocated to military equipment and to the support of subversive elements abroad.

When Edmund Burke was discussing the dangers of having too much faith in theories, he said, 'I mean always a weak, erroneous, fallacious, unfounded or imperfect theory; and one of the ways of discovering that it is false is by comparing it with practice.' If you take social and economic conditions together, it is obvious that in practice Marxist states are less economically successful and less socially humane than any comparable bourgeois democracy. No wonder Professor Kolakowski described Marxism as 'the greatest fantasy of our century'.

At least in pre-Marxist days the idea of sin was fairly well understood and evil was personified in the Devil and those individuals who behaved in a patently evil way were possessed of the Devil and invited to repent. Today, ever since

Marx's generalisations, evil is embodied in certain classes, in institutions, corporations, general groups or simply in vague concepts such as capitalism, imperialism or colonialism. All these things have to be hated and destroyed and it is an interesting fact that in Marxist literature there is hardly ever anything to be admired, except its own heroes, nothing to be loved, except the State, and nothing to be respected except force. No wonder the creative arts are politically controlled, culture is put into museums and religion so discouraged.

It is understandable that convinced Marxists should adopt such attitudes: their whole ideology is based on the idea that any degree of force, subversion, terrorism, persecution and dishonesty is justified in achieving and maintaining the dictatorship of the proletariat. In theory, yes, but in practice it merely maintains the dictatorship of bureaucracy. Thercfore it should come as no surprise that when political power is acquired by violent and dishonest means the power so gained will be exercised in the same way, and it is not limited to purely internal application.

If the subjugation and control of foreign governments is not imperialism, my understanding of the term must be at fault. Yet Marxists use words such as 'imperialist' and 'colonialist' as terms of invective while they themselves are busy subverting or acquiring control of other countries. This is rather like Humpty Dumpty's attitude to words: let them mean what you want them to mean. In the Marxist dictionary 'peace' might appear as 'surrender on my terms', 'liberation' as 'military occupation', and 'détente' as 'you must be nice to me but I can do what I like to you'.

The full extent of Marxist subversion and violence is impossible to describe but it is estimated that in the fifty years between the beginning of the Russian Revolution and 1967 the number of deaths directly attributable to Marxism or

Communism from execution, man-made famine, imprisonment, slave labour and civil and international warfare, could not be lower than 70 million. Solzhenitsyn has suggested that, as he put it, the 'cost of socialism' is over 110 million lives.

Compared to these staggering figures the incidental hardships caused by even the most corrupt bourgeois capitalist democracy pale into insignificance. It all seems such a very long way from what Marx was convinced would be an ideal society. For instance, in *The German Ideology* he wrote:

> What I like about the Communist society is that it will make it possible for me to do from day to day just as I feel, to hunt in the morning and to fish in the afternoon.

What is positively frightening is the dogged determination of so many otherwise intelligent people to confuse intention with reality and to prefer a myth and a fraud to the glaring evidence of fact. This obstinate and blind commitment to an ideology, which in practice produces little but hate and violence, is well illustrated by Beatrice and Sidney Webb. These two well-meaning, incorruptible, bourgeois idealists visited Russia during the height of the Stalin purges and the forced collectivisation of agriculture. In *The Mainstreams of Marxism* Professor Kolakowski describes this programme as 'probably the most massive warlike operation ever conducted by a state against its own citizens', and again 'an unparalleled orgy of bloodshed and hypocrisy'. Modern estimates put the death toll in Russia during the years 1932 and 1933 at 10 million, with a similar number imprisoned in concentration camps. It is not as if these monstrosities were not there to be seen. Bertrand Russell saw them and reported what he saw. Yet the Webbs apparently failed to notice.

They produced an enormous book declaring that the Soviet system was the embodiment of man's dearest longing for justice and happiness. This remarkable aversion to reality seems to be just as strong today among those who obstinately believe that the best prospects for the future of humanity lie in the glorification of hatred and violence.

This, it seems to me, is Marx's legacy to the world. For love, tolerance and compassion he has substituted hatred, envy and oppression. For honesty and justice he has substituted the interest of the party. Although it is a sad commentary on human nature that so many people are eager to adopt such doctrines of violence and conflict, there is one thing we must all learn from Marx. It is now more important than ever that we learn and understand the guiding principles of our own system, if we are to make it fulfil our ambitions to live in freedom, in harmony, in prosperity and in justice.

The second aspect of this chapter on conflict harks back several years to an address I gave in the series of 'One People Orations'.* I suggested then that unity was an unnatural state of existence; and if we start with the idea that absolute unity is neither desirable nor even practicable, we are left with the problem of deciding which forms of diversity are acceptable and beneficial, and which are responsible for open and harmful conflict. For it is quite possible for any number of divisions to exist between people which do not necessarily lead to a dangerous state of conflict. Diversity is in fact essential to human progress. Diversity of opinion and experience is an important factor in human intellectual evolution. Furthermore, without diversity there would be no choice, and without choice there is no freedom. We should

* Westminster Abbey, 12 July 1972: 'The Nature of Conflict'.

not imply that diversity is undesirable, but that it is those consequences of diversity leading to emotional antagonism and outright physical conflict which are to be deplored.

The trouble starts when communities become fearful that others may compromise their way of life, their language, beliefs or means of livelihood. These divisions are not necessarily the creation of some deliberately malign influence. They are simply the by-products of geography and the general principle of natural selection; and to isolate those divisions which lead to open conflict we must establish those areas of conflict which man has inherited from pre-history and those which are the result of more recent intellectual development. Furthermore, we have also got to take into account that it is possible for one man to belong to a number of different recognisable groups at the same time, some of which may be ancient and some modern.

For example a man may be of African origin, born and living in the U.S.A., belonging to the Roman branch of the Christian church, a member of the Democratic party and a supporter of one of the National League baseball teams. Each one of these categories puts him in direct contrast to someone in an alternative category of the same sort. His African origin is in contrast to someone of European origin. He is a citizen of the United States compared to someone with Mexican nationality. He is a Christian as opposed to a Muslim. He is a Roman Catholic as opposed to a Seventh Day Adventist. He belongs to the Democratic party as opposed to the Republican party, and he supports one baseball team in preference to another.

It is the diversity of groups within the broad categories which continues to give rise to the tensions, jealousies, and outright conflict, and which has plagued the world for so long. Ironically, it is mutual hostility between the different groups which within each group can often create or strengthen a sense of unity and cohesion. Where this becomes particularly strong, it may well lead to various forms of aggression and violence. On the other hand, I think it is reasonable to suggest that the early Christian Church was given great strength by the hostility of its oppressors and that its subsequent success was due in no small measure to its energetic and aggressive missionary zeal.

Many people have been tempted to blame aggression for all forms of conflict. There is a risk, but not an inevitability, that aggressive behaviour by groups or by individuals will lead to conflict. The displacement, geographically or economically, of one racial or tribal group may well proceed peaceably enough, just as there are instances of conflict where the aggressive instinct is not strictly to blame. The great migrations of nomadic tribes from central Asia certainly led to conflict with neighbouring people, but the movement was due to increasing numbers and lack of grazing rather than to any inherent aggressive instincts.

The lesson of history since very primitive times is that the most prevalent sources of conflict are the racial and eventually the national differences between people. Once our primitive ancestors began to domesticate themselves and thereby increase their chances of survival and improve their standards of living, it seems likely that they had to spread out and eventually settle in a variety of climatic and geographical environments. These dispersed settlements probably became and remained isolated from each other through hostility towards any new settlers. Isolation is known to be a very important factor in the development of races, so that even after a relatively short period of time the isolated groups became physically and culturally adapted to their own special conditions. The longer they remained isolated the greater became their distinctive features, just as communities which were constantly being overrun by others or were themselves constantly in conflict with their neighbours were less likely to develop distinctive characteristics.

It is easy enough to see how the different races developed as a result of the isolation of communities from each other, but it is quite a different matter to decide exactly what factors constitute the differences between the races of Homo Sapiens.

The obvious answer is that races can be distinguished by their physiological differences, of which colour is probably the most noticeable. However, colour alone is not enough. There are any number of races with black skins and just as many with brown, yellow or white skins. Physical type might be another criterion, but here again there are several races with very similar physical types. You have only to look at the European races. Geographical distribution might be another method, but throughout history both groups and individuals have moved great distances and, provided they are not physically recognisable by colour or type, they quickly become assimilated into their new community and join that nationality. The English are a very good example: as a race they have absorbed a number of different migrations, and yet remained English. At the same time it would be inaccurate to suggest that only the people living in Scotland or Wales are Scottish or Welsh. At one time differences in diet, climate and isolation made physical differentiation possible between quite close neighbours but today it would take a very careful examination to discover any comprehensive physiological or morphological differences between the Scots and the Welsh. Yet the Scots and the Welsh are regarded as separate races.

It looks therefore as if there is no single factor which

constitutes race, but rather that it is a combination of a number of factors, including colour, physical type, geographical distribution and, perhaps most important of all, a common culture. People who share language, literature, social structure and customs, religion, diet and special artistic tastes and talents, will inevitably feel a greater sense of cohesion, whatever their physical type, even if they are not all living together in one geographical area. Strictly speaking the Welsh race is a cultural entity. Indeed I suspect it would be virtually impossible for a Welshman to prove that he was Welsh in any other way. Much the same could be said about the United States and particularly of such concentrations of population as New York where the 'melting pot' principle causes remarkable physical and cultural transformations.

This raises the very interesting problem of the Black Americans. Most of them have lived in the New World for many generations and have become culturally entirely different from the people of their place of origin. In the United States they speak English, belong to one of the group of religions, and – culturally – have helped to create a specifically American style of music. They have fought for their country and served it in every possible way. In Brazil their language is Portuguese and they have contributed to the creation of a specifically recognisable Brazilian culture. But for their colour they would be indistinguishable from all the other inhabitants in their own nations of the New World. It would therefore be fair to say that recognisable American races have developed and that they are made up of a wide variety of physical types.

The really important factor is the cultural attachment which people feel most strongly and wish to defend most energetically. Naturally race plays a more important part and is more easily defined if the members of a nation or community share the same colour, physical type and geographical concentration as well as culture. In a mixed community with graduations between the extremes of colour, this factor is less obvious.

In effect this means that where conflict occurs it is due to a will to protect territory, or culture, or both, and that the physical characteristics of race have very little to do with it. Indeed civil wars, which are frequently more bitterly fought than national wars, usually result from ideological differences.

Once communities became established, the difficulty of maintaining ordinary movement and communication between the specialist races ensured that each developed its own language. This division by language is probably the second most significant division, because it inhibits the easy and natural exchange of ideas. It destroys the one thing which has given mankind such a tremendous advantage over all other living things.

It was the development of intellect that began to open up a whole new range of opportunities for conflict. Where formerly conflict arose over possession of land and resources, it could now be generated by diversity of religious and political theories. Indeed the main area of human conflict has been shifting gradually away from issues caused by practical circumstances towards intellectual and emotional causes. The development of intellect has brought with it a self-awareness and therefore a far more intense appreciation of beauty and horror, love and brutality, joy and misery. This in its turn has made it possible to conceive the idea of good and evil and what ought to be done. It has also brought to light an in-built conflict in ourselves between what we conceive to be right and what our inclination would have us do.

Until speech and intellect had evolved to a decisive stage, the development of human races, communities and culture was dictated by factors outside the conscious control of mankind. The communities responded more or less blindly to the external forces of nature. Conflict took place over clearly defined issues and was accepted as a natural part of existence. Gradually, however, the power of speech became more sophisticated and with it the power to observe, discuss and reflect. It also made it possible to influence men's emotions and imagination. By this time the adaptation to climate and function had gone so far that the infant struggles of the intellect were bound to be influenced by the particular situation and race of the thinkers. Religious and philosophical ideas which they developed were separated from each other by the differences which had already grown up between human communities; but, even so, in many ways they exhibited a remarkable basic similarity.

It is noticeable for instance how many have shared the same progression of ideas, from superstition through hero worship, divinely inspired leadership, organised religion, priest-kings, emperor gods, to the revealed religions of the present day. The woods, as it were, look remarkable similar; it is only when you get down to studying the trees that the differences become apparent. But these intellectual, as opposed to practical, differences not only exist, they have been, and still remain, one of the most divisive influences on mankind. The irony is that so many of these philosophies were developed by the most thoughtful and intelligent men as the supreme ideals for all mankind. They still remain potentially the most unifying ideas in this present day.

Indeed it is to these thinkers that we owe our concepts of good and evil, right and wrong, and the vision of better human behaviour. It is therefore hardly surprising that religions and philosophies have captured so completely the imagination and devoted loyalty of so many people. However, the very strength of their attachment has only served to increase their suspicion of those following a different system. It is this very loyalty which is largely responsible for the unhappy conflict between religious beliefs and particularly between the various branches of the Christian faith. Human characteristics of a very ancient origin are still able to overcome the unanswerable logic of the brotherhood of man that love is better than hate.

Conflict between rival groups is only one side of the picture. Conflict for power and leadership within the groups is equally important. The struggle for individual supremacy is probably even older than the family Hominidae. As a source of human conflict it has certainly not diminished with the development of human civilisation, but the rules governing the conflict for leadership have gradually become more sophisticated. In theory, at least, it is no longer a case of brute force and unscrupulous cunning although at times of severe tension brute force may still decide the issue. At other times people have come to accept the rule of laws and constitutions as a means of settling internal struggles for power without resorting to blows. The whole purpose of what we describe as the democratic system is to allow a change of government without the need for violent revolution. The whole purpose of law and justice is to protect the weak from the strong, the individual from the gang, and the minority from the majority. Indeed without justice and law civilised life cannot exist, and democracy, including peaceful protest, cannot work.

The system may well not be perfect, but at least it is a good deal better than any system where power is gained by subversion, terrorism and violence and maintained by the same means. Any system based on a rational philosophy and voluntary acceptance is better than one based on expediency and imposed by force.

With the gradual improvement in technical ability and organisation, coherent human communities grew from tribal groups to city states and eventually to supra-national empires. In order to achieve this sort of political growth, there had to be three essential ingredients. First, an efficient military and civil organisation; second, a strong religion or philosophy, voluntarily accepted; and third, wealth.

In the course of time, as we know only too well, the pursuit of material wealth, both personally and nationally, has become one of the most important factors in human motivation. This factor, coupled with much older behaviour patterns, established new systems of power and social structure. The influence of wealth has become steadily more important as the opportunities for making it and using it have increased; and the inevitable consequence of this has been the development of theories for the creation and distribution of wealth, and the protection of property. As people have ranged themselves behind one theory or another, so these economic theories have become the basis of conflicting political systems and emotional attachment, and so to yet one more division.

The arguments rage about two questions. How should wealth be created and how should the wealth be distributed? The argument may take many forms but this is what lies at the heart of the problem of industrial relations and the economic and social management of national affairs.

When it comes to the matter of ideas, the facts have never been allowed to influence the argument. Christianity is not alone in making martyrs of those who sought truth by scientific means. In the U.S.S.R. the science of genetics was gravely retarded when Lysenko's pseudo-science was officially supported by the Government and many genuine scientists were hounded, arrested and imprisoned. Even today there is really nothing better than an uneasy truce between science and religion, causing unhappiness and uncertainty among many people who feel they have to make a choice between the two. This is particularly ironic as both claim to be seeking the truth. Both must share part of the blame. Science has advanced so far that there is a serious knowledge gap developing and this lack of general understanding is leading to a fear of science which might soon give way to hostility. On the other hand, the religions suffer because even the limited understanding of the non-scientific is sufficient to expose many inconsistencies which are inevitable in ideas based on the knowledge available three or four thousand years ago.

There was a time when the whole explanation of man and his position in the universe was based upon divine revelation. In the rush to give everything a scientific explanation and to put down all human behaviour to natural and evolutionary causes, we must be careful not to ignore or underrate the tremendous power of the human intellect. People are influenced as much by the attitudes, motives and conclusions of both ancient and current philosophies as they are by the ascertainable facts, so that the resolution of the conflict between science and religion is essential if man is to make any further intellectual progress. As de Tocqueville said: 'Men will not accept truth at the hands of their enemies and truth is seldom offered to them by their friends.'

We can see the outcome of all these divisions around us today. We can recognise only too easily the racial tensions which were born in prehistoric times. We know what emotions are aroused when any language appears to be under threat. We can see the tensions which have developed out of attempts in different parts of the world to arrive at a satisfactory religious sytem. Most obvious of all, perhaps, are the national, economic and political tensions which have now arisen from isolation, lack of communication and the search for wealth and prosperity. Throughout all these factors we can trace the element of fear and its corroding effect upon human relations. The only certainty about this planet is that change will go on, sometimes faster, sometimes slower. It so happens that we are living through one of the most dramatic periods of change the world has ever known. This is certainly creating new tensions, but it is also breaking down many of the old divisions which have been plaguing man's peace and security since he became capable of worrying about them.

The size of political entities has always been limited by the field of consciousness of its members. For the first time people are beginning to be conscious of the whole world and its place in the solar and stellar system. Political consciousness has been going up the scale from 'my family', 'my city', 'my country', to 'my world'. Perhaps some future generation may be able to say 'my universe'. If consciousness on this scale can be combined with love and concern then there is real hope.

If we are to ensure that future generations can enjoy the full natural diversity of the earth it is going to mean a concerted effort on a scale never before attempted. It is going to mean a radical reorientation of the vast power of modern technology. Much of it will have to be diverted from the creation of wealth to the more pressing problem of the survival of man. If we are to succeed in this we must certainly be agreed about the ends, although we do not have to adopt identical means.

Now, for the first time since mankind took off on his materialist spree, there are signs that human, ethical and moral values are coming to be seen as more important than the most glittering products of engineering genius. This is no reflection on the engineer, it is just that we have been making the wrong demands on him. For too long we have been obsessed with the excitement of new technical developments and forgotten that it is people and the living things of this earth that are more important. We have rated computers above compassion, machines above mercy, and telecommunications above human relations. We have forgotten that in every age the great human civilisations have depended far more upon emotional inspiration than upon the standard of the plumbing. We cannot blame any of the practical inventions of man as the cause of human conflict. For that we have got to look at man himself.

It is becoming increasingly obvious that it is people and not machines that we should be worrying about. We should be discussing motives and ideals, incentives and behaviour, crime and morality, faith and inspiration, because it should be only too obvious that the juggernaut of technological progress can only be kept under control by people. The way in which the control is exercised depends upon the standard of human ideals. If tribalism and commercial greed are the dominating motives, or if we accept human conflict as inevitable, then the juggernaut will surely destroy its master. If it is concern for continuing human welfare through an objective understanding of human nature, respect for the natural environment, and a firm belief that this planet should be left to our successors not too badly damaged, then I think there is a chance that the juggernaut can be brought to serve its master.

Mankind has entered upon a totally new era of experience

within a totally new environment, which he has created for himself. There will be more technological developments to come but it is unlikely that any will be as radical as those which have appeared within the last two generations. From now on we will have to concentrate on devising a philosophy which takes account of these new technological and intellectual environments. We need a new vision of the future and a new interpretation of the ancient truths, set in the context of man's present and likely future situation.

There is every reason to be hopeful. The immensely long story of the family Hominidae has been one of slow but gradual improvement. The process of domestication which started so long ago made it possible for mankind to multiply in the way he has and it has steadily improved the standards of material existence for immense numbers of people. The potential for spreading this improvement more widely is in our hands. Improvement has also taken place in man's intellectual and philosophical existence, and this has made the dangers of conflict and the advantages of cooperation increasingly apparent.

The spread of education is gradually creating the situation where all mankind can share the same understanding of the world and universe around us and of the human situation within it. There will doubtless always be a proportion who will enjoy reverting to standards of behaviour which even our remote ancestors would have found idiotic and revolting, but surely it is not too much to hope that more and more people will come to realise that it is men and their behaviour, their emotions, their conflicts, and their ideals which govern the future. Rational man knows this and tries to act upon it, but those who allow themselves to be blindly driven by uninhibited human nature are quite capable of destroying us all.

This is nothing new; in fact the most dramatic clash between reason and bigotry in all history, as far as Christians are concerned, was when Our Lord was crucified. His life and His teaching, and the example of the lives and teaching of other great thinkers in other parts of the world, have provided the genus Homo with all the clues which it needs to control its conflicts and to safeguard its future. The question still remains whether we can make an adequate response.

# 2
# Truth

# Truth

Our elaborate legal and judicial system has as its purpose the establishment of a truth that is known to exist, in that something was done and some person or persons were responsible. Criminals, for reasons of self-interest, tend to be reluctant to admit the truth about their misdemeanours and sometimes suspicions, for various reasons, fall on perfectly innocent people. Our judicial need is to establish the 'truth, the whole truth, and nothing but the truth', and our system has evolved over many centuries of experience of human nature. But when we are confronted with conflicting evidence we can at best be dealing with probability – even 'beyond all reasonable doubt' is only an extreme state of probability. That the judicial procedure occasionally miscarries tells us more perhaps about man's ambivalent attitude to truth than about any weakness in the system.

In scientific work the problem is more complicated because the nature of the truth not already established by experiment can only be guessed at and the guess subsequently proved or disproved. If, as frequently happens, the proof of a theory is not acceptable, the publication of the results of research and the subsequent criticism of its methods and conclusions should be sufficient to ensure that any wholly or partially false information does not come to be accepted. But there is a very serious weakness in this argument because the author of the paper and the critic both have vested interests in the subject. The same factors which may have led the one astray might conceivably have led the other from the narrow path as well, and probably the most powerful of these factors is wishful thinking or the desire to make the results of research conform to the postulated theory.

In scientific research the issue is likely to be resolved by further experiment until a number of workers are able to repeat experiments which can only allow for one conclusion or which establish one or more indisputable facts. Yet there are any number of cases of papers purporting to prove one thing or another which are then taken up by the popular media and any falsehood they contain is spread far and wide. Once they have acquired popular acceptance it becomes a great deal more difficult to refute and correct them. In the rather more obscure researches in pure science, this may not be, practically, very important. For example, it is very unlikely to make a very great difference to humanity if the theory of continental drift or the properties of black holes, or the exact size and speed of micro-particles, are not exactly correct. On the other hand it matters a very great deal if the research results have any commercial or industrial value. Such cases as the supposed relationship between dairy products and cholesterol, or cyclamates and cancer were responsible for huge financial gains and losses in spite of the fact that the original work was either suspect or misleading.

There is a risk, too, in a commercial world that scientists working for the vested interests will exercise themselves over legal safety standards but leave to others investigations that might prove commercially inconvenient. In the early days of interest in the conservation of nature, for instance, there was much circumstantial evidence that certain agricultural chemicals, particularly those described as persistent, were having a serious toxic effect on wildlife. It was perhaps not altogether surprising that certain scientists were in no great hurry to establish the facts. This is not actually telling a lie but equally it is indifference to the truth.

Another area where such research can be of popular concern was instanced by that very dilemma which, in part, prompted this choice of subject. There was at the time a great debate going on about the use of fluoride in drinking water to prevent dental caries. This effect was pretty well established but there was then the counterclaim that a higher rate of cancer occurs in those communities where fluoride is added to the water supplies. A very serious allegation and yet the evidence was so uncertain that even courts of law found it difficult to establish the truth. This was largely because those who argued for and against tended to be committed to a particular point of view. Furthermore it was one of those arguments which could not be settled by the facts alone but by what was acceptable in practice – similar to the debate about the use of nuclear reactors to produce electricity. Will it ever be possible to produce the sort of facts that will convince one side that it is safe or the other that it is dangerous? There is no evidence to suggest it has been dangerous in the past but it is quite another matter to predict whether any part of the process or disposal of waste will not be dangerous in the future. I have a feeling that wishful thinking is not going to help the process of establishing the truth in this case.

In both scientific and particularly in academic work the greatest danger lies in drawing conclusions from false or incomplete evidence. Science at least has a sort of self-correcting mechanism. Even Lysenko could not get away with his rubbish indefinitely in spite of the backing of an absolute dictator. However, when it comes to such things as political theories, histories, economic commentaries and all the other intellectual activities which require judgement to be exercised in the selection of facts, and where objectivity, or the lack of it, exercises a dominating influence on the final conclusions, truth need hardly figure at all. In these cases it is much easier to make the results of research conform to a predetermined theory. Adam Smith, Karl Marx and Maynard Keynes presumably had roughly the same facts at their disposal but the conclusions they came to were totally different. They were each presumably convinced that theirs was the whole truth, but who is to say which had more of it than the others? Unlike the legal process or in science where the ultimate purpose is to establish the truth, there is really no satisfactory formal process whereby the truth of academic works can be assessed. There is no ultimate criterion to decide between the prejudice of the author and the prejudice of the critic. Even if you say that in such cases the relative success of ideas put into practice should be the guide, it is quite obvious that none of them is wholly successful for everyone all of the time; so that the judgement of what is successful is also bound to be subjective, and that is not a good guide to the truth at any time.

The trouble is that the more difficult it is to prove the truth of any particular idea, the more the issue becomes one of emotion. The great religions of the world are each convinced that they understand the true significance of life and death and that their particular interpretation of the mystery of the universe is the true one. It has to be said that most, if not all, of them are committed to the concept of an ultimate truth and the absolute importance of trying to find it in all things, and in this respect they score pretty heavily against the political and other wishful thinkers. But religious convictions are probably even more difficult to prove than political theories and it is perhaps for that reason that attachment to them is governed by such intense emotion.

There are, it seems to me, certain factors in the search for truth that need to be taken into account. There is first of all the process of the selection of facts from which some sort of conclusion can be drawn. Major falsehoods can be created simply by assembling only those facts which tend to prove the hypothesis while ignoring all the others. This can be done just as easily by scientists as by academics (though while the scientist is likely to be found out and his hypothesis disproved, the academic may well get away with it). In consequence, there are many people who come to accept a false hypothesis simply because the arguments and the selection of supporting evidence are to their taste. Their approach – frequently, dare one mention it, a product of university brainwashing – is 'My mind is made up; do not confuse me with the facts'. The phenomenon occurs because apparently new and unconventional ideas are inclined to be accepted as glimpses of the truth simply because they appear to be new and unconventional. But originality and conventionality are subjective. What seems new and exciting to some may be old hat and unsatisfactory to others.

The dissidents in the comrade countries and the Marxists in the other countries are good examples of this situation, with both of them using their own evidence and experience to prove what is wrong with their own establishment. They both go on to imply that there are such things as utopian solutions, in spite of thousands of years of history to demonstrate the patent absurdity of such a claim. Neither side is ever likely to agree that in practice some systems are further removed from utopia than others. Once committed no one likes to have to admit that he might have been wrong; and without the ability to speak freely there is no way of telling whether acquiescence implies support or opposition.

If getting at the truth is a problem, it is far more difficult to correct misconceptions or to get people to see that some of their cherished beliefs have little or no foundation in established facts. Preconceived attitudes are easily acquired. Teachers, usually unwittingly, but sometimes wittingly, can allow their enthusiasms to give greater or less emphasis to certain factors in their subject which can have quite important consequences. Then, as everyone knows, leaders in a subject are capable of setting fashionable theories. Elliot Smith and his theory of the diffusion of culture is an example of an eminent scientist and a strong personality dominating the attitudes of a complete generation. The trouble is that truth to many people is not what is, but what they believe it to be or what they would like it to be. One might describe the attitude as a 'Flat Earth Society' mentality. The difficulty is to convince people about unpalatable truths: from the Old Testament prophets to the present-day dissidents, history shows it to be an uncomfortable pursuit. It is not easy to apply rational criticism to a fashionable concept and hope to be accepted by the so-called Establishment. But in science, if not in politics and economics, false conclusions never survive for very long.

Finding the truth is the purpose of all science. For scientific purposes I am not convinced that a definition of truth is all that significant. It seems to me that science is not a thing, it is a method, so that the way you search for truth is really the most important factor. If you use the scientific method you are more likely to find an aspect of real truth than if you rely on intuition or guesswork or any other system; and the scientific method – and life in general for that matter – requires three things: technical knowledge, personal observation and judgement, and moral standards. To take a very simple example: if you want to discover the truth about the structure of a fly's wing you need to know how to operate a microscope. Having got the fly under the microscope the next step is to observe, to notice significant details and to judge whether they are relevant or irrelevant. But the moral consideration is probably the most important because both technical choice and personal judgement are influenced by moral standards. Without absolute honesty and objectivity in the approach to the search for truth the results will be misleading, which is worse than not finding anything at all.

This is probably self-evident but what may not be so obvious are the factors which tend to modify or subvert absolute honesty and objectivity in science. Perhaps the classic situation arises from an attempt to prove a strongly held theory. It is extremely difficult to set up an experiment, or to embark on a series of observations, without tending to favour the presupposed answer. No one can ignore a perfectly obvious and blatant failure, but it is not so easy with, let us say, marginally ambiguous results. And if the whole experiment is biased in favour of a particular solution, then ambiguous results are even more suspect.

There are also other and more subtle obstacles to finding the truth. For example, at one time religious beliefs inhibited a great deal of research. One can imagine that, quite apart from official pressures, the religious convictions of the research worker himself might encourage him to accept certain evidence more readily than other perhaps more theologically awkward results. The Copernicus and Darwin cases may perhaps have succeeded in setting science free from the constraints of theological convictions, but we now have the equally damaging phenomenon of political convictions creating preconceived answers or encouraging politically acceptable solutions. Hitler, for instance – fortunately for us as it turned out – would not allow nuclear research to continue because the leading research workers in that subject were

Jewish. There are similar instances in Soviet Russia of which the Lysenko story is probably the best known. Today we, in the so-called free world, have to face the challenge of genetic engineering and decide whether to impose limits on this line of research. The choice is a very difficult one as the future of all life on this planet depends upon the freedom of inquiry, yet this needs to be balanced against the moral and practical consequences of the power to interfere with natural genetic processes and even to create quite new processes.

There is probably not very much anyone can do to improve his powers of observation and judgement. Practice helps; so does remembering how important they are. But they require a certain talent which is given to some and not to others. Technical knowledge, on the other hand, can be acquired up to quite extraordinarily high standards. This is one of the principal responsibilities of schools, colleges, universities and a mass of other organisations. The argument is not the possibility of imparting technical knowledge, the argument is simply about what technical knowledge is necessary for anyone hoping to earn a living, or simply to exist and appreciate life in a technically advanced community.

This is not to oversimplify the function of our educational system. We have always had a touching confidence in the ability of education to solve all our problems. People seem to forget that education is double-ended. There is the teaching end which demands both a talent for teaching and a relevance of what is taught; and then there is the learning end which expects both the will to learn as well as a talent for the subject being taught. Without these conditions education as such can achieve nothing.

There is also what to my mind is a misconceived idea that all education can be delivered in one package covering school, university and specialist training. Paradoxically, the more experience you have of a subject the more you can learn about it. Learning against a background of no experience means that there is no way of assessing the importance or the relevance of what is being taught. A lot of people can navigate a ship along a difficult coast in the comfort and safety of a classroom; the problem is rather different on the bridge on a wet and stormy night. Learning against a background of practical experience, on the other hand, makes it far easier to appreciate how the new knowledge fits into the real life situation. Management, in particular, is to do with human nature and the interplay of human and individual personalities. In these circumstances, personal experience of human behaviour is an essential prerequisite to the study of particular techniques and the many specialised branches of management.

As a matter of fact, I have come to suspect that our great success with machines and mechanical and electronic systems, together with our academic and analytical approach to economics, has led us to believe that all systems, including those in which people are involved, are capable of being controlled by a rigid and comprehensive formula. Management of people cannot be reduced to a formula; human personalities and circumstances vary much too much for that. There are, however, certain rules of human nature which must be learned and observed and I suspect, even more important, there are certain attitudes of mind – moral standards perhaps – which are just as essential for a successful manager as a knowledge and understanding of the techniques of management.

This problem of moral standards is a great deal more difficult and their importance within the education process is frequently overlooked. Yet it has been the experience of every civilisation that standards of honesty, integrity, compassion, manners and personal behaviour, which are acquired during the education process, are far more significant than the standards of academic achievement. A society of brilliant barbarians would soon end in chaos. Even the less brilliant can all become clean, honest and well-mannered and that would be a big step towards a more civilised society.

It is easy enough to recognise the need for absolute honesty and integrity in relation to science, but I do not believe that you can switch moral standards on and off at will. There cannot be (though of course people try) any such thing as a separation within the individual between public and private morality. In the same way there cannot be any separation between religious truth and scientific truth. They may well be dealing with different aspects of the subject, but it is not possible for something to be true in a scientific sense and not true in a religious sense. Equally, theology cannot claim something as true which can be disproved by scientific methods. That is not to say that theology is prevented from claiming that it can provide a theory to explain things for which science can provide no explanation.

Indeed I would suggest that theologians and scientists are each aiming at the same goal, although taking different routes, and they need to recognise this if we are ever to restore a unity of outlook on all moral problems. If there is to be any separation between theology and science, then let it be decided by function and not by forcing people to choose between conflicting demands. Absolute standards of honesty are required by science, but there are many other moral issues in life which are the proper concern of theology.

I believe there is an essential link between pure science and the human experience to be found in the study of the natural sciences. They are subjects of interest in themselves but they are also the foundation for understanding man's place in the universe. It seems that we have become so dazzled by what we take to be our own creative genius that we have neglected, or forgotten, or ignored the infinitely complicated web of nature which sustains our very existence. This suggests to me that of all the subjects taught in school the natural sciences, and natural history in particular, are the ones to which all children should be exposed. After all, humanity is a part of what de Chardin called the biosphere – in other words the living world and its environment – so there really is a good case for giving natural science the same level of importance as literacy and numeracy. If you come to think of it a lot of people survive without being able to read or write or do arithmetic, but no one has thought of a way of living without a body. It is rather a sad commentary on our contemporary priorities that of all the functions of our bodies the only one that schools feel it worth bothering about is the reproductive system. Each of us is a component part of living nature anyway, and unless we can learn to understand living organisms we are very unlikely to be able to understand ourselves or anything of man's situation.

A background of knowledge of the natural sciences is essential for all technologies and most vocations and professions. I am not suggesting that the classics and humanities are not entirely respectable and worthwhile academic subjects – they always have been and they always will be – but I am suggesting that to be without a basic understanding of the scientific method, and without any appreciation of the scientific basis of the modern technologies, is to be part-educated, almost intellectually crippled. I believe, however, that the case for natural history, and particularly biology, as a core subject can be amply justified. It can be justified from the scientific point of view because natural history teaches the basis of the scientific approach to all subjects and also because it emphasises the decisive value of observation and judgements. I think it can also be justified from the moral point of view because in contrast to mathematics, for instance, which depends on accuracy and only admits right and wrong answers, the right answers in natural history, namely the truth, can only be found by the deliberate choice of rigorous honesty and objectivity. It is the truth that here concerns us. I have said that it is not always self-evident; it is frequently deliberately obscured and distorted for all sorts of reasons. This means that it is not simply a matter of being aware that there is such a thing as truth, but that it also needs to be diligently sought after through the maze of self-interest, prejudice, preconception, wishful thinking and frequently impressive but irrelevant facts. Some matters, of course, will always be subject to opinion and preference. But one thing I should describe as self-evidently true: peace, love and beauty cannot be obtained by falsehood.

# 3
# Clashes of Interest

# Clashes of Interest

Although this chapter is concerned with conservation, it illustrates the way in which difficulties can be caused by the clash of perfectly legitimate and well-meaning interests. Many people seem to think that the conservation of nature can be achieved quite simply and easily. To them it is just a matter of stopping greedy industrialists, preventing the killing of any wild animals and turning all forests and wilderness areas into national parks. It may be easy enough to put it like that but to carry such a plan into operation is a practical impossibility. The only way to cope with the problems of conservation is to try first of all to understand their cause.

This is substantially, but with some amendments, the text of the Fairfield Osborn Lecture I delivered in New York on 1 October 1980.* The late Fairfield Osborn was a man after my own heart: a great enthusiast for conservation, a fearless exponent of the dangers of the human population explosion, and an enlightened and progressive President of the New York Zoological Society. I saw in a short biography of him that 'his childhood interest in a private menagerie grew to encompass a broad range of environmental activities'. I am not sure whether this means that his father had a private zoo, or whether, and I think this is more likely, he was one of those small boys who delight in carrying about with them a

* With thanks and acknowledgements to the New York Zoological Society.

menagerie of various animals and insects in pockets and matchboxes, and whose bedroom is more like a miniature zoo. They are a trial to their mothers, a fright to their aunts and the despair of their teachers, but they often grow up to be great men.

I was fortunate enough to be able to attend the inaugural dinner in New York at the launching of the United States National Appeal of the World Wildlife fund in 1962. I cannot now remember all the details, but I do remember getting into diplomatic hot water for suggesting that a certain country with a vast and rapidly expanding population did not really need the assistance of the products of rhinoceros horns for certain natural functions. As it happens the poor rhinos ran into another problem, finding their horns in great demand for making handles for ceremonial daggers in certain parts of the Arabian peninsula.

It is instances such as these – and there are any number of them – which are liable to turn otherwise calm and sensible conservationists into militant fanatics. This is unfortunate for two reasons. First because anger usually makes people rude and insulting, and that is certainly not the way to win friends and influence people. Secondly, anger makes people thrash out blindly in all directions so that if they actually succeed in making any impression at all, it is more by good luck than good judgement.

In anything to do with conservation, I believe it is particularly important to keep cool, read the World Conservation Strategy, think deeply and be particularly careful to identify the interests of the people and groups most directly involved. It is then a matter of dealing with each situation in the most appropriate and effective way. Uncompromising confrontation may work sometimes but any reasonably intelligent person is more likely to respond to explanation and a well-argued case for conservation. However, before you can make the case it is vitally important to have a clear conception of the purpose, and therefore of the priorities, of conservation. We all claim to be concerned about conservation, but the word means different things to different people.

Some are more interested in the conservation of the human and built environment, others take it to mean the conservation of nature and the natural environment. Since man is a part of nature certain issues and situations are common to both, but while it is reasonable to worry about the human environment and desirable to try to create a satisfactory state of existence for ourselves and for those animals and plants which serve our needs, the conservation of the wild forms of life and of the wilderness areas, which constitute the natural environment, is a rather more difficult issue. The problem arises because in the majority of cases involving the conservation of nature it is the activities of particular people which pose the greatest threat to nature and, consequently, a balance has to be struck between their interests and the claims of the natural world.

But, much as some people would like, it is really not possible to prevent every instance of human interference with the natural environment or every case of the exploitation of wild populations. It may well be distasteful to kill baby seals, but provided the species as a whole, or any branch of it, is not threatened with extinction itself, or is threatening the extinction of another species, it is not a conservation problem. It may be a moral problem, but it cannot, for example, rate a higher priority than the protection of a species from extinction, even if the threat to the survival of a species is posed by such morally less offensive activities as drainage schemes, commercial fishing or the cropping of forest areas.

Although the ordinary processes of nature have long term

effects on wildlife and the natural environment, by far the most immediately damaging effects are caused by human activities. The point to bear in mind is that all human activities have their origin in the decisions of individuals or groups of individuals. It is also worth remembering that these activities are seldom motivated by malice, vindictiveness or cruelty towards nature. Nearly always the damaging consequences of the activities derive from ignorance, self-interest, thoughtlessness or simple irresponsibility.

Detached and analytical intellectuals tend to rationalise the whole thing by saying that someone, or something, called 'man' is responsible for all the problems. How often one hears enraged conservationists talking about 'man' being greedy, irresponsible, self-indulgent or guilty of any other sin they care to mention? I have to admit that I have done it myself. It is so easy to pick on 'man' as the culprit, it sounds rather grand and impressive, but in reality the expression 'man' is a convenient but meaningless generalisation. Lumping the world's four billion people into one category is patently absurd, and if the term is used to include all men who have ever lived, it is even more ridiculous.

It seems to be that as conservationists we need to be a great deal more realistic about human behaviour and human emotions, reactions and prejudices. Not everyone has the same characteristics but people can be expected to respond in certain ways to certain stimuli. One of the most difficult tasks you can attempt is to get someone to accept your point of view and to act on your advice without the use of force or other pressure. Taking human nature into account is for us of the utmost importance because in the final analysis nature is at risk through the conflict of human interests.

Although ignorance is not strictly speaking a characteristic of human nature, ignorance of nature is certainly a characteristic of most people and the cause of a great deal of the trouble. It is easy enough to say that adults ought to know better, but if you come to think of it, every child is born totally ignorant and, what is more, there is a new crop of them every year, of which an increasing proportion will be born and brought up in cities. It is true that they all have instincts and talents but these are not much use to them until they acquire some knowledge and experience. It is quite unrealistic to suppose that children growing up in an urban situation will acquire the same knowledge of the natural environment as children growing up in the country.

When the children from the poorer districts of London were evacuated to the country at the beginning of the last war, it was said that many of them refused to drink milk, which they had seen coming from a cow, because they believed that the real stuff only came out of bottles. This is an extreme case, but many bright and intelligent city children go on to become managers, leaders in their professions and creators of opinions, and if they remain ignorant of the basic concepts of conservation it will only be a matter of time before they find themselves in conflict with their better-informed fellow citizens.

Once upon a time it might have been an idea to appeal to parents to give their children the facts about our natural environment and to try to make it possible for them to be exposed to the grandeur, beauty and awesomeness of nature; not in some flabby romantic sense, but in both its harsh and tender reality. Unfortunately, in this modern enlightened world, the experts seem to discourage the idea that parents should have any responsibility for the education of their children. One English headmaster was recently reported as saying: 'I am not sure that parents know what is best educationally for their children. They know what's best for them to eat. They know the best environment they can provide at home. But we've been trained to ascertain the problems of children . . .' and so on.

However, judging by the appalling ignorance of so many people about the processes of nature and the frightening, but usually unintentional, damage being done to the natural environment, it does seem that the professional teachers, psychiatrists and sociologists, who control education in these days, are not particularly interested in the principles of conservation.

A deer-stalker recently said to me that he had come to the conclusion that the more people were educated the less common sense they seemed to have. He then told me of the two students who went climbing in the [1979] winter in the hills near his home in Scotland without telling anyone where they were going. Four days later he found them dead from exposure. If people are sufficiently ignorant to allow nature to kill them, it is hardly to be expected that they will understand the principles of conservation.

This same sort of ignorance is capable of putting the whole future of our world at risk.

As Fairfield Osborn saw so clearly, the greatest threat to the future of the earth is the unchecked human population explosion. This is likely to increase the number of living people from four billion today, to an estimated six billion by the year 2000 on a planet which has no prospects of increasing its size to accommodate them. Some might argue that 'man', and presumably 'woman' in this case, was being guilty of gross irresponsibility. That obviously is not true because a great many parents are highly responsible and furthermore, fortunately perhaps, there are a large number of people who have no children at all. The trouble is that there are so many females of breeding age who are either ignorant or irresponsible, or sometimes both ignorant and irresponsible, and so many men to encourage them to be irresponsible. Before anyone jumps to conclusions, let me say at once that I am not discussing the morality of contraception, I am merely drawing attention to the obvious fact that if only 90% of all female children born alive survive to breeding age and then have more than two or three children each, it can only feed the population explosion.

This is a classic case of a conflict of interest between individual parents, who naturally feel entitled to have as many children as they please, and the world at large which patently will not be able to support a natural world as well as to feed and house a vastly inflated human population.

Paradoxically, it has been the success of the medical and agricultural sciences which has made the population explosion possible. It is one of the laws of nature that any population will increase to consume the food and the space available unless checked by disease or famine. The conflict arises because while everyone with the slightest spark of humanity clamours for more food to feed the growing number of under-nourished people, conservationists are loud in their protest about modern farming methods, and the reclamation of wilderness areas for agriculture. But attacking agriculture is rather like blaming 'man' again. Who identifies with agriculture? It is an abstract concept, useful maybe for economists and for the civil servants and scientists who work in government departments of agriculture, but I doubt whether farmers and landowners feel that it applies to them personally, and I am quite certain that the very large number of peasant and subsistence farmers in the Third World are completely unaware of the argument anyway. In any case farmers have their own conflict of interest to resolve. They have to farm for profit or, put it the other way, they obviously cannot afford to farm at a loss. Therefore they are unlikely to be sympathetic to any form of wildlife which in fact, or in their belief, is likely to reduce their yields.

Some farmers and officials of Ministries of Agriculture have to cope with more subtle conflicts. For instance, scientific investigation has established that wild badgers in England and wild opossums in New Zealand are liable to infection by the bovine tubercle bacillus and in their turn they are known to spread tuberculosis to domestic cattle. The disease can then be passed on to the human population through the cow's milk, although pasteurisation has greatly reduced the risk. It is, of course, fairly easy to control the disease in cattle by the simple expedient of slaughtering the infected animals. Strangely enough this raises no protest, presumably because they are domestic animals. However, it is an expensive method and not unnaturally farmers get a bit discouraged when their herds are constantly re-infected and liable to slaughter. But what to do about the wild badgers and opossums? A similar policy of eradication by slaughter is hotly opposed by protection societies, even though it would also benefit both the wild species in the long run. Indeed both badgers and opossums are at greater risk of decimation by the further spread of tuberculosis throughout their populations than by a policy of slaughtering the various pockets of population suffering from the disease.

It is not that farmers do not understand the principle of conservation. After all they practise it all the time. They have to keep back seed and breeding stock for next year's production; they have to provide a habitat for their stock and they have to feed it. In fact many of them take a lot of trouble to make life possible for a large number of wild creatures without great cost to themselves and at the same time they make their farms that much more interesting and satisfactory places to live on. There are any number of examples in many parts of the world of farmers who do just that and still manage to thrive economically.

Much the same applies to foresters in the developed countries. Of course some animals are nuisances and any species can become a pest if its population gets too big, but there is a great difference between trying to exterminate a pest and learning to live with a nuisance.

But the conflict of interest becomes much more intense in the so-called developing countries. To the eyes of conservationists the great natural rain forests are objects of beauty and delight and the habitat of a vast range of plant and animal life. They are also vital components of the world's climatic conditions and the carbon-dioxide/oxygen cycle, but to the government of these countries, struggling with internal hunger, poverty and unemployment, with external debt and with a plethora of well-meaning advisers and foreign aid programmes, the forests represent wealth in a fairly easily convertible form. Anyone who feels like persuading them otherwise must proceed with caution and much tact.

The conflict between cash and conservation also extends into the wildlife of many developing countries. Horns, tusks, skins and meat are all tempting resources for poachers, and particularly in situations of political instability or government lethargy, cash wins fairly easily. Furthermore, it is no use believing that the designation of national parks and the introduction of legislation will necessarily solve the problem. Unless the parks are properly managed and the legislation effectively enforced little significant conservation is achieved. In mid-1980 the U.S. World Wildlife Fund appealed for $1 million to protect African elephants against ivory poachers. It is estimated that between 50,000 and 150,000 elephants are being killed each year.

A rather different conflict exists in the development of other forms of natural resources. Water in particular seems to have the most extraordinary effect on engineers. They either want to keep it in dams and reservoirs, or they want to drain it away to the sea as quickly as possible. The single-mindedness with which hydro-electric engineers, municipal water supply engineers, irrigation and drainage engineers go about their business is most impressive, and I am quite sure that they do not set about their work with the sole intention of destroying the natural environment and removing the habitat of wild species. It is not that they just do not care, it is simply that many of them do not know, and a little politely offered information is more likely to have an effect than a military confrontation. After all, they are just as capable of understanding the value of conservation as any of us.

Ten years ago the River Thames in London was virtually lifeless, today it is once again being used by migratory fish and much other wildlife. This rehabilitation of a severely polluted waterway stands as a good example of what can be achieved, at quite a modest cost, by understanding and co-operation between conservationists and various specialist engineers. The difficulty is that engineers have to reconcile the demands of their communities with the needs of nature, and that is not at all easy when angry rate and tax payers are demanding service for their money. As a matter of fact I would not be at all surprised if the same people who complained about inadequate water supplies and sewage services were also devoted conservationists giving both time and money to persuading 'man', or perhaps 'agriculture', to mend their ways.

In these days of threatened energy shortages it is tempting to suggest that more power should be produced from sources of ambient energy, such as windmills, solar collectors and further hydro-electric developments. Some of the schemes might be quite harmless and some even beneficial to the natural environment, but others could be extremely damaging. It is impossible to generalise and in the end the decisions will depend on the good sense and judgement of the individual engineers and administrators responsible for the generation of energy. Both their good sense and their judgement would be vastly improved if they had a greater understanding of, and sympathy for, the problems of nature. They therefore need at some stage to be made aware of the damage their developments are capable of inflicting on ecosystems and habitats.

One of the most potent threats to wildlife is pollution. We all know that. But it is no good leaving it at that. Human activities produce many different kinds of effluents but not all of them are dangerous to all forms of wildlife in every case. In fact, pollution, in the sense that an effluent into the water or into the air or into the earth causes damage to plant or animal species, has a greater variety of causes and effects than any other of the major man-made threats to the natural environment. It can be anything from untreated human sewage discharged into a river to highly toxic chemical wastes discharged from some industrial process. It is its immense range and the general ignorance of the subject which makes pollution so difficult to control, and unless each case is considered within its particular parameters I really do not believe it will be possible to make much useful progress in coping with the problems.

The waste and sewage disposal authorities have to resolve a particularly awkward conflict of interests. Their problem is that treatment costs money and no elected body ever wants to ask for more money than the community believes to be absolutely necessary, and if the community is unaware of the dangers of discharging untreated sewage into rivers or estuaries, it is unlikely to press local governments to spend money on treatment works. The inhabitants of the smaller and more rural communities live rather more closely to these mundane affairs and are consequently more likely to appreciate the problems than the people living in the great metropolitan conurbations, most of whom are blissfully unaware of the damage caused by the disposal of their wastes and sewage. Furthermore pollution control is a relatively recent idea and not easily accepted by organisations which have been able to do as they pleased for a great many years.

This also applies to many industries, but here again not all industrial processes produce pollution and even different companies performing the same processes do not all produce the same amount of pollution. In some situations the effluents can be discharged without damage, while in other cases companies, of their own volition, take appropriate measures to prevent their effluent doing any harm. The difficulty today is to identify the particular company which is causing damage and then to discover which individuals in that company have the necessary authority to take steps to prevent it. Then again, in some cases these individuals will accept the conservation argument and do something about it, in other cases they may not be so cooperative. It is therefore important to devise a system which penalises those responsible for the damage they do and so provides an incentive to control pollution. As all industrial companies have to live with the market system, there is no reason why the price mechanism should not work in such cases, provided of course that a cost can be put on the damage done to wildlife and the natural environment.

Even more intractable is the international pollution conflict. The River Rhine is an international waterway flowing through many different countries, each of which applies its own, and in some cases that means no, pollution control. The power stations on the east coast of Britain have high stacks to carry the effluent clear of the population. However, the prevailing wind is from the south-west and much of the sulphur dioxide comes down and affects the forests of Sweden.

Difficult as it may be to control pollution, it is probably no harder than trying to contain the damaging effects of activities which, performed by individuals on their own, are quite harmless in themselves, but which can cause devastating damage when endlessly repeated by a great many individuals. Recreation is a good example. It is not that any particular individual is responsible for damage, it is simply the cumulative effect of, for instance, large numbers of tourists, which can cause serious disturbance to wild populations, the erosion of the land by killing off the vegetation with too many tramping feet, and pollution by litter. The same applies to the taking of game animals and fish, and the collecting of birds' eggs, butterflies and rare plants.

The difficulty about resolving the conflicts in this area is that there are so many individuals involved, and few of them belong to what might be called 'single communication groups'. They do not belong to any particular club or society, they probably do not even read the same newspapers or watch the same television programmes, so that there is a real problem of getting the conservation message across to them and explaining to them how it is that the cumulative effect of many people indulging in the same activity can adversely affect the natural environment. This is a particularly difficult problem because so many people confuse their appreciation of nature and the wilderness with the conservation of the natural environment. The two, unfortunately, are not synonymous. For one thing the beginning of conservation is self-restraint not self-indulgence.

The irony is that measures to protect particularly sensitive wilderness areas frequently have the effect of attracting more visitors. It would obviously be desirable, but probably not practical, to restrict entry to such areas to those who are prepared to join a particular organisation. This would put them into a single communication group and give them a proprietary interest in the area, and therefore make it possible to influence their behaviour.

Hunting and fishing for recreation are also activities which in moderation can be harmless, but if pursued to excess can do really serious damage. It happens that the hunting and fishing laws in the U.S.A. enshrine the principle of free-for-all, although there are, of course, bag limits. There is nothing wrong with that. However, it is one thing to say that it is legally free to do something, but that does not mean that it must also be economically free to do it. People are free to form manufacturing companies, but that does not mean to say that those companies should be free to cause damage by discharging dangerous effluents. In principle there should be an economic inducement to hunters and collectors to conserve the objects of their interests rather than to exploit them. If this cannot be done by allowing them proprietary rights over certain areas, then at least they should be required to become subscribing members of an organisation which was itself committed to the conservation of their quarries.

Commercial sea-fishing provides some good examples of the effect of applying these principles. A few years ago, the waters around Iceland beyond the three-mile territorial waters limit were free-for-all, and the consequent overfishing reduced the stocks of fish to a dangerously low level.

Then, after a considerable struggle and two so-called 'cod wars', Iceland succeeded in gaining proprietorial fishing rights out to 200 miles, and it is now in a position to conserve the fish stocks in that area. In effect, Iceland now farms those waters which used to be free-for-all and consequently exploited without restraint.

In the North Sea almost the reverse took place. The whole of the North Sea was thrown open to the fishermen of all the members of the E.E.C. just at the time when fishing techniques were becoming increasingly efficient. In consequence it was over-fished, resulting in a severe restriction on the taking of most species of fish and much unemployment among fishermen. In effect no country has any proprietary rights, and therefore there is no inducement for the fishermen to conserve fish stocks; and, apart from the E.E.C. itself, there is no fishing organisation to which the fishermen can belong which has the purpose of administering a conservation policy in their interests.

Whaling also illustrates the difficulty of reconciling the purely practical issue of the conservation of species from decline and possible extinction with the moral and emotional issue of killing animals. In the case of whales the technique employed to catch them could hardly be termed humane. In any case there is inevitably greater sympathy for large animals and what might be termed 'cuddly' animals than for what many consider to be pests and 'creepy-crawlies'.

Furthermore, good conservation practice may entail what is termed 'culling' and this can cause serious conflict between people otherwise devoted to the principles of conservation. Take, for example, the case of the vicunas in Peru. The scientists working at Pampa Galeras claimed that there were 44,000 of them and that they needed to be culled. However, an aerial survey commissioned by those who thought that they should not be culled put the figure at between 15 and 18,000. In my experience anyone who tries to restore peace between arguing conservationists usually comes off worst of all. Nevertheless, in spite of all these difficulties, membership organisations and voluntary work are absolutely vital to the conservation movement.

The protection or the conservation of nature or care for the environment, whatever you like to call it, is not a new idea. What is new is the vastly increased number of people all over the world who are taking an active interest in it. The world of nature is based on the process of evolution. It may take a very long time to change us genetically but as we are a thinking species we are also influenced by the evolution of ideas. The evolution of the conservation idea is giving nature a chance to survive human interference but it may well also turn out to be one of the most important factors in the survival of the species Homo Sapiens itself.

# 4
# Individual and Community

# Individual and Community

The nineteenth century saw the transformation of what was a predominantly rural and agricultural society into an urban and industrial way of life. Where the former was influenced by such things as the climate, the passing of the seasons and the rhythm of plant and animal life, the new pattern had its roots in technology and science, and in cheap fossil fuels. New factors such as pay packets and balance sheets, charts of economic statistics and self-made men assumed great importance. The rural scene may have looked feudal to the casual observer and in retrospect, but in fact the structure revolved around a remarkable degree of interdependence and a social hierarchy with an almost infinite number of grades and permutations. Indeed nearly everyone had his unique function in the community. This is reflected to this day in the structure of those old market and country towns which have not been totally inundated by industry. In addition, whatever other divisions there may have been, the whole population acknowledged that they were all equal in the sight of God, although not perhaps in any other way.

This view of pre-industrial life may sound rather too romantic for strict accuracy. I do not pretend that life had no problems at that time. The important point is that industrialisation brought a completely different way of life and a different set of problems. The industrial operation depended on the employment of an unusually high proportion of unskilled workers within the factories. The new industrial towns offered an escape for the larger numbers of the poorer agricultural workers as well as for the young looking for adventure, but while the change offered new and unlimited opportunities sometimes for the energetic and enterprising, the developing urban industrial structure created quite different divisions between workers, managers and owners. The pattern of the housing for this growing urban industrial working class inevitably resulted in a new form of structural segregation in the industrial cities, with many of the social consequences we see today.

The first half of the twentieth century saw the fruits of industrial production reach all levels of the community. The technological progress which brought electricity and the telephone, sewage systems and improved water supplies, also brought mobility and the things which went with it; and the expectation of more to come. Furthermore the industrial community itself developed from a mass of unskilled, inexperienced and relatively uneducated workers into a much better educated, better technically equipped, more politically conscious and more socially ambitious group of people doing a very wide variety of technical and intellectual jobs.

These fundamental changes to the national structure, caused by the shift of population from country to town, are directly reflected in the evolution of political attitudes. It is no coincidence that a whole new crop of ideologies has been stimulated by the spread of industrialisation; but whatever political ideology has been developed and subsequently superimposed, every so-called developed country also exists in a state of what might be described as industrialism. And by that I mean that most of our social and practically all of our intellectual attitudes today appear to be deeply influenced by industrial standards and criteria. There is a tendency to assess education by its 'throughput' – if you look at any reports on education you very often see that term – almost regardless of its content; and housing is judged by its cost per unit, almost without regard to its suitability.

Industrialism has also created its own brand of economics, the economics of growth and size, and this has resulted in a direct economic competition between governments, less bloody than outright warfare but conducted with much the same ruthlessness. As an abstract concept the economics of scale make sense, but when you insert an intelligent and alert human factor into the equation, bigger in the economic scale inevitably means bigger human and social problems. For one thing the bigger an organisation the slower it is to respond to changing circumstances and, even more important, to specific human concerns. And this seems to be reflected in the apparent correlation between size and industrial unrest.

A new philosophy of life has come into being – or perhaps industrialism has simply buried the old philosophies under the doctrine of expedient materialism. Individuals are now required to conform to rigid standards of mechanical efficiency, and the ultimate human aspiration becomes nothing more than conformity to the industrial herd. Man is no longer seen as an image of God with each individual unique in His sight. Concern for the development of the individual is pushed aside by the more practical need to wind up the human intellect like a clockwork mouse, and then to let people loose to perform and apply their talents in strict proportion to how much money they are allowed to earn.

One of the most important consequences of industrialism is quantification. Every factor considered to be important in the daily lives of people has to be measured. Industry, which in its turn gave rise to technology and applied science, depends upon calculations of all sorts, measured by numbers and best handled by computers. None of them allows for human idiosyncrasy or ambition. Improvements in the collection of facts and statistics may help to diagnose faults and failures but that is a long way from finding an appropriate cure for the human problems encountered in a modern industrial society.

Quantification has created a fetish for statistics that has spilled over into fields which used to depend upon judgement and a sensitivity to the problems, frustrations, ambitions and successes of people. Counting heads, classifying groups, working out averages and percentages, drawing conclusions and predicting trends from computerised intelligence now tends to become the substitute for humane government and considerate management alike. Dictatorship by statistics is probably the ultimate bureaucratic paradise, but government is not about figures, it is about human beings. Management is not about statistics, it is about actual people.

Craftsmen from the very earliest times have organised themselves into guilds. The City of London Livery Companies remain to demonstrate the important part which these organisations played in the government of the pre-industrial chartered towns of England. Under industrialism this system has been greatly expanded and extended. Today it includes special unions for the unskilled or unspecialised workers and the Trade Union Movement has developed as a whole on a national scale. It also includes trade associations and employer organisations which were part of the guild system and have developed separately from the Trade Union Movement.

The influence of these organised groups has become statistically very much more important, and this has not gone unnoticed. The natural reaction of many of the professional classes, the doctors, engineers, farmers and a whole host of other occupations and professions, has been to form their own groups for self-protection against the modern statistical approach to social, industrial and political issues. This fragmentation of society does not seem to be the most likely way to arrive at rational solutions for national problems.

Quantification has also tended to reinforce generalisation. Judging by the attention they receive, one might believe that concepts like the national economy, industry, labour, commerce, science, or technology, all have an existence of their own, but this is simply because certain aspects of them can be reduced to statistics. All these things are figments, they have no real identity. They are convenient terms; nothing more than collective nouns, and they can never represent the individuality of the people involved in them.

This de-personalisation and secularisation is one of the most unfortunate features of industrialism. Even Marx, who might be described as the prophet of industrialism, acknowledged the part religion played in the lives of people caught up in a, for him, de-personalised system. He said 'Religion is the sigh of the oppressed creature, the heart of a heartless world, the soul of a soulless environment, it is the opium of the people.'

That is obviously still true today and I suspect that there are many people in the countries which adopted his ideas who would also echo those sentiments. But I think it would be true to say that Marx recognised, more clearly than most, all the worst features of industrialism and from this he drew the conclusion that the whole system was at fault. I believe an equally valid conclusion would be that the people most actively involved in it were at fault. And I believe that we can, and indeed we must, bring some sort of humanity into industrialism, whatever political system is adopted.

In pre-industrial days a whole elaborate structure of

religious, legal and moral constraints and institutions was developed to keep uninhibited human nature within the bounds of civilised behaviour under the circumstances of society at that time. Although industrialism was a practical revolution, it also released a wholly new range of human energies. It does not follow that the old institutions are no longer relevant, it means that the new intellectual environment and the attractions of material progress are creating a new set of moral and philosophical problems for the old institutions which constitute a very grave challenge to their influence.

The most serious difficulty seems to be that politics are taking over from religions. Government is no longer satisfied with the almost neutral concern to make it possible for people to live in peace, security and freedom. It has become government by party for party with the additional conviction that it is possible to control human morality and behaviour by legislation. It is all very well to say that this is justified because it is in the interests of the common good. The fact is that the liberty of the individual is a vital part of the common good also.

It is patently impossible to achieve the public good by coercion or by discrimination against law-abiding individuals whatever minority group they happen to belong to. It may also be held that more controls give the individual greater freedom in the form of freedom from want; but there is a very great difference between freedom from something and freedom to do something. People living in a desert have freedom from rain but without rain an industrious farmer cannot raise any crops.

The evident success of industrialism in raising material standards demonstrates that if people are prepared to give up some of their individual choice and responsibility, by working for an efficiently managed, profit-orientated project, and by being members of a trade union, they can expect great material benefits. The trouble is that the promise of benefits makes people overlook the loss of choice and responsibility which inevitably follows. It also obscures the fact that nothing short of a totalitarian government can itself attempt to generate the wealth necessary to provide the benefits.

But if management can make profits with a well paid and well looked after work force, why should not a political government be able to do the same thing for the nation as a whole? Why not indeed? Except we should not forget that a citizen has always looked to his government to protect his personal liberty, security and peace and to apply the necessary constraints to the excesses of human nature and the power of factions in society. He accepts personal sacrifices for the common good but he does not expect to be managed by his government as if all citizens were nothing more than so many units of labour in a collective enterprise.

Since time immemorial there have been arguments about the relative importance of the individual and the State. There is no doubt that in moments of desperate national crisis a people united behind a leader have willingly given up much of their individual liberty and have achieved great things. But the crucial moment always arrives when the people become disenchanted with the inevitable constraints they accepted during the crisis while the leader is inclined to remain determined that they are still essential for survival. And there may also be a difference of opinion about what constitutes a crisis in the first place. In the British democratic system this situation is resolved by a relatively peaceful process, but in other systems it is inclined to lead to the excesses of dictatorship or violent revolution.

I believe that one of the great dangers of industrialism is that it is liable to bring together some very potent and powerful forces against the liberty of the individual. Secularisation, de-personalisation, generalisation and computerisation between them could well destroy what is left of the individual personality. I believe that this should be our point of departure when we begin to consider the future of industry, or indeed the future of all our institutions.

It must begin with the individual and the family as the foundation of society and we must get it firmly fixed in our minds that all the trappings of our social, religious, political and industrial systems exist for the sole purpose of allowing life to be as tolerable and as civilised as possible for the individual and the family. Only if we start from here are we likely to get our directions right. If things can be got right for the individual I believe the rest will follow. If the interests of the individual are ignored we shall end up with a form of tyranny which other societies have suffered under at various times in history.

The first and most important consideration is this: that every individual is unique. The world may confront us with common problems but each individual reacts to the problems in his own way. At the heart of all social structures and political systems is the nature of man. The process of evolution and natural selection has given us various features and instincts which we all share. This is our human nature, and try as we may to sublimate it to rational intellectual argument very few of us will ever completely transcend it.

So the very first rule of any system or organisation is that its whole structure must be compatible with a realistic understanding of human nature, giving full encouragement to its beneficent and creative qualities while providing the necessary restraints on its less admirable characteristics.

History provides more than sufficient evidence that crooks can flourish under any system, and they are more likely to do so in a system devised by idealists than in one devised by realists.

No system can work for long, even if it seems to be rationally perfect, which ignores the forces of human nature. Adam Smith saw this very clearly two hundred years ago.

> The man of system . . . seems to imagine that he can arrange the different members of a great society with as much ease as the hand arranges the different pieces upon a chess-board. He does not consider that the pieces upon the chess-board have no other principle of motion beside that which the hand impresses upon them; but that, in the great chess-board of human society, every single piece has a principle of motion of its own, altogether different from that which the legislature might choose to impress upon it. If those two principles coincide and act in the same direction, the game of human society will go on easily and harmoniously, and is very likely to be happy and successful. If they are opposite or different, the game will go on miserably, and human society must be at all times in the highest degree of disorder.

It is the principles of motion of the single pieces on the 'great chess-board of human society' which concern me here. I believe that there is no viable approach to an industrial future unless these principles are understood. The force behind all the motions is the need to provide the necessities and satisfactions of life, more usually and simply referred to as making a living. The purpose of making a living is to live a good life and if possible to do better. It is a means to the end of affording and equipping a home. It is a means to the end of providing for a family, and there can be no more laudable ambition than to bring up and educate children to become responsible and decent citizens.

It is a means to the end of achieving a degree of financial independence and security against a rainy day; against sickness and old age. It is clearly the duty of governments to provide a safety net for those who fail or who are unable to look after themselves, but that is no reason to create obstructions for the more fortunate individual whose prime ambition has always been to provide for family, health and old age, the voluntary support of charities and the personal involvement in cultural activities.

There is much talk about participation in decision-making at work, but work is only one factor in human existence, even if it is a very important factor. Participation as a citizen is far more important because people have more in common as householders, parents, patients and pensioners than they do as workers, and their need to exercise their responsibilities as citizens is as important, if not more important, than the need to be involved in decisions about their work. Of course there will always be a hard core of people who cannot be responsible. It happens in all walks of life and at all intellectual levels, but it is patently a denial of liberty to allow any social system to develop in a way which withholds from an individual the opportunity of becoming a responsible member of the community.

Any individual or group of people with the power to make decisions also has the responsibility for the consequences of those decisions. Technical and managerial problems are significantly different from decisions about issues which affect people personally as householders and parents; but both are part of human existence.

If people are not trusted they have a way of becoming

untrustworthy; if they are not encouraged to be self-reliant they can easily lose their initiative and be satisfied with dependence. If working for a living is a common factor in the lives of most people, working in industry is just one opportunity to make a living. Industry is therefore a means to an end and not an end in itself. This means that industry can only flourish if its component parts are able to flourish, and they can only flourish if the people working in them are allowed to flourish. Again Adam Smith had the right words for it two hundred years ago:

> The natural effort of every individual to better his own condition when suffered to exert itself with freedom and security is so powerful a principle that it is alone and without assistance not only capable of carrying on the society to wealth and prosperity but of surmounting a hundred impertinent obstructions with which the folly of human laws too often encumbers its operations.

So far as industry is concerned the first thing to do is to identify and remove some of those 'impertinent obstructions', which, I suspect, have also suffered from inflation in the last two hundred years. Clearly we have got to be more realistic about them, remembering that they can safely be removed without weakening the safety net for the helpless or the unfortunate. The development of various schemes for greater participation in decision-making in industry should also be judged from the point of view of removing 'impertinent obstructions' to the individual's effort to better his own condition.

However, more important than participation from the individual's point of view, I suggest, is cooperation. In the end all enterprises depend on the quality of the decisions taken and no one in his senses is going to be satisfied to work for an organisation which takes decisions which lead to failure. The fact remains that no enterprise can hope to succeed without cooperation between everyone involved. Furthermore this is the only way in which each individual can hope to better his own condition. It is worth noting, too, that it seems that cooperation is much easier to achieve in the smaller enterprises where there is little or no distinction between manager and worker anyway. It is a fallacy to assume that all managers and all workers in every enterprise, whatever its size, have exactly the same industrial relations problems.

Seen from this angle the future of industry takes on rather a different perspective. Industry has become the primary opportunity for people to make a living and to improve their condition. Therefore the criterion of success is the prosperity of all the people engaged in it and associated with it, and not some complicated set of figures about an abstract Gross National Product or balance of payments. The art of government is to make individual ambitions and self-interest coincide with the national interest.

As I see it, the future of industry depends fundamentally upon the future of the individual and not the other way round. It is not some vague concept of industry which needs attention but the well-being of individuals as workers, managers, shareholders, consumers and as citizens. The first essential therefore is that people should be as free as possible to make a living in their own way and encouraged to make the very best use of their talents and enterprise. They should have as much independence and responsibility as possible as householder, parent, patient and pensioner, they should have every opportunity to participate in making the decisions which affect them as citizens, and they should have the greatest freedom of choice in recreational, cultural and personal affairs.

It is too glib to assume that simply because adults have the vote the present local and central government arrangement provide these opportunities. It may be economically necessary to have professional legislators, but this is a wholly different concept from the idea of representation of citizens by citizens. It may be administratively convenient for such matters as health, culture, water and recreation to be put in the hands of councils, committees and boards whose members are almost entirely nominated, but this is not what I understand is meant by participation. After all, the resources which make public services possible are derived from the fruits of the work of individuals.

It is obviously essential to have an efficient civil administration, but if it becomes too big and cumbersome it is likely to defeat the very purpose for which it was established, which is to help and encourage individuals to be self-reliant and responsible citizens. It is certainly not intended to harass and confuse them. There may have been a time when bureaucratic paternalism could be excused, but by far the great majority of the people of this country today have shown that they are capable of self-control and personal responsibility. The style of industrial management is already beginning to change and it remains to be seen when the style of bureaucracy will adapt to the new conditions.

Governments are obviously required to maintain a balance between the various factions in society, not for the benefit of the governments or of the factions, but for the protection of the individual's freedom, security and rights before the law. There seems to be a danger that this primary duty may come in conflict with its growing responsibilities as an employer. Substituting Parliament for shareholders does make it more difficult for Parliament to treat all sectors and sections of the State with complete impartiality.

I believe that any approach to the future of industry which ignores the place for the individual is a waste of time. We should not forget that the people of industrialised countries have shown quite remarkable talents over the centuries. When these talents were allowed to be devoted to useful and productive ends, as Adam Smith said, 'the game of human society' went on 'easily and harmoniously'. On the other hand, when the talents and gifts of individuals are driven into time-consuming, unproductive and conflicting activities 'the game will go on miserably'.

# 5
# Community Health

# Community Health

We live in what is termed a permissive society, yet in practice I doubt whether any previous generation in the so-called free countries has ever lived under such a thick blanket of restrictive legislation and bureaucratic control. In theory we have been freed from stifling conventions and old-fashioned obligations, while in reality we have gradually been losing individual responsibility and freedom of choice. We seem to have achieved the remarkable situation where nearly half the population is telling the other half what it should be doing and thinking, and checking up that it is doing it. Of course, we all *like* to think that we know better than the next chap, but there is very little evidence to justify this claim and it is no reason for us to use legislation to force him to do what we may think is good for him.

The point is that the mentally and morally fit do not need to be directed, controlled and checked morning, noon and night because morality, amongst other things, is to do with the ability of individuals to identify the difference between right and wrong. Many people confuse morality with convention and maintain that it is established merely so as to allow the species or the community to survive. Survival may well be dependent on convention, but sheer survival may also justify violence and aggression. Right and wrong derive from an understanding of good and evil and that in turn depends upon belief. There has never been a major civilisation in the history of the world that was not based upon a philosophy of good and evil quite beyond and outside the ordinary practical conventions.

All the great religions set out their own arbitrary ideas about good and evil and the extent to which these ideas influence their followers depends entirely upon how strongly their followers believe in them. If you remove the religious concept of good and evil you are left with purely pragmatic and expedient conventions. Conventions may decide that stealing and dishonesty are anti-social and should be punished as a deterrent, but only morality can make people refuse to steal, and desire to be honest. Convention may establish methods of settling disputes but only morality can persuade people to love one another or to honour an undertaking. Only a moral imperative can persuade husbands and wives to be faithful to each other.

There is today a way of expressing things which gives the impression that it is organisations and groups, rather than individuals, that are required to have moral attitudes. We talk about 'the Government', 'the Employers', 'the Unions', 'the Media', 'the Church', and so on, as if the collective group had some sort of separate existence and character of its own. We say, for instance, that the Government is being honest or dishonest, or that the Church should have an attitude towards racial discrimination, whereas the fact is that each of the groups is made up of individuals and the attitudes and activities of each of the groups are decided by the individuals who make up their membership.

Joining a Christian church does not make anyone a Christian. It is the other way around. A number of Christians have to join together before a Christian church can be formed. A government is not a tyranny or a democracy or corrupt just because of the way the constitution is written: it is made one way or the other depending on the morality and the convictions of the individuals within it. I daresay even the Communist system would be tolerable if all government officials had the character and morality of angels. A police force is neither brutal, oppressive, considerate or polite simply because it is required to enforce the law. It is the individual policeman in every rank and his personal moral standards which is the determining factor. And the same applies to every group.

It follows therefore that moral fitness depends upon the conviction that certain things are good and honest and that other things are vile. These have to be personal convictions, they cannot be established by convention or by legislation. A person may be physically fit and mentally fit and still be an accomplished criminal or terrorist. Neither of these activities may lead to lung cancer or heart disease but both can end in premature death or lengthy imprisonment, both of which could be described as definite health hazards.

Morality is not only to do with attitudes. An understanding of good and evil should also lead to better standards of personal behaviour. Looked at from the other side, it is only too apparent that so-called revolutionaries who reject moral and behavioural standards as reactionary and old-fashioned end up with the standards of terrorists where violence and the infliction of pain, suffering and death are causes for pride and satisfaction. The victims have good reason to know that terrorism is a serious health hazard both for the physical damage as well as the worry and anxiety it causes.

As I have tried to point out, conventions are not the same thing as moral standards. For instance, in a community of criminals it is unconventional to be honest, while in a law-abiding community it is unconventional to be a crook. Furthermore, in this age of mixed-up economic values any man who does not follow Keynesian principles and tries to live within his means, who does not borrow money but saves and invests for the future, is definitely unconventional if not positively eccentric.

But quite apart from conventions, communities also display recognisable symptoms of health and disease. In certain communities there is an exceptionally high incidence of vandalism, mugging, drunkenness and drug taking. Even if not all the members are involved, that community as a whole can only be described as sick, and no matter how healthy an individual member may be in every other respect he cannot avoid being contaminated by the sickness of his community. In other communities business prospers, the arts flourish and no one need fear for their life or property. I think it would be fair to describe such communities as healthy.

Very slowly we are beginning to learn about community sickness and to understand some of its causes. We are beginning to understand that when mistakes are made in large-scale planning and macro-economics the consequences show up as community sickness. We are slowly learning that the apparently magnanimous provision of facilities for educational, cultural or recreational purposes is not entirely satisfactory unless the people for whom they are provided also have some proprietary interest in them. We are also discovering that the only hope for the healthy individual or family to escape the corrupting influence of a sick community is to pack up and leave, although this only makes matters worse for those who remain behind.

This understandable instinct to turn one's back on a sick community is reflected, too, in public attitudes to crime and punishment – a crucial aspect of the sickness. The whole subject of crime and punishment tends to be ignored by those who are lucky enough not to be affected by it, and the views of those who are rather naturally tend to be influenced by on which side of the law they find themselves. Meanwhile the pressure for reform seems to concentrate on the processes of detection, judgement and punishment without regard to the environmental factors encouraging crime. Or at least these factors are taken to be extenuating circumstances rather than as active causes of crime. Whatever the case, the figures are pretty discouraging. With this avalanche of lawlessness threatening to engulf our civilisation, the more discussion there is about 'social control' of crime the better.

Every community in history has had to draw up a list of things which its members were required not to do. These rules may have been based on different practical, philosophical or religious considerations, but in effect breaking the rules of the community is crime. However it is all very well to make the rules; the next problem is to decide what to do about those who break them.

The first thing is to try to catch them and to make absolutely certain that only the offenders are caught and that the innocent are allowed to go free. The police and the courts exist for this purpose, and there is little doubt that in this country at least they perform their function. But what to do with those who have been proved beyond reasonable doubt to have committed the offences? I imagine that the concept of rewards and punishments must have been well understood even in the most primitive communities, although the exact purpose of punishment has never been completely clear.

If you punish a child or an animal for doing something wrong, the purpose is to remind it not to do it again. The punishment of criminals, on the other hand, quite apart from the 'don't do it again' element, can also be used as a deterrent to would-be criminals. If a potential criminal knows what the penalty is going to be for a particular crime, he can work out the risk of being caught and whether the price is worth it. Then in some cases exemplary penalties are given, which is really an escalation of the deterrent, but such a punishment always strikes me as rather unjust as the culprit so penalised cannot really be held responsible for others committing the same offence.

There is one further purpose of punishment, and that is to exact retribution, the Mosaic concept of an eye for an eye and a tooth for a tooth. This type of punishment has virtually disappeared from this country with the abolition of corporal and capital punishment for crimes of violence and homicide. But whatever the theory it is self-evident that there are many cases where no sentence is effective either as a punishment or as a deterrent or as retribution.

Those who commit offences or crimes for political, religious or conscientious reasons are seldom influenced by fear of punishment, even if it is capital punishment. It simply becomes martyrdom. Neither does it have much effect on those of temporarily or permanently unsound mind.

Whether the exact purpose of punishment is ever resolved or not, it seems to be generally accepted that something of the sort is necessary. But this still leaves the problem of what form punishment should take. Over the years, and for various reasons, the only punishments left to our courts are fines and prison sentences – in other words, deprivation of property or deprivation of liberty. Courts, of course, have other forms of treatment such as probation, deferred sentence, conditional discharge and community service orders, but these are threats of punishments rather than direct penal sentences.

Of the two punishments fines are more or less effective depending on the wealth of the offender, while prison, on the other hand, may be an effective punishment for those of sound mind, but unfortunately the deprivation of liberty also has to be used to protect society against highly dangerous or mentally disturbed offenders, neither of which are likely to respond to punishment or rehabilitation. Furthermore, and this is a very real problem, the view that offenders are more in need of help and rehabilitation than of punishment means that prisons have come to be used both for the purpose of deprivation of liberty as well as for the training and rehabilitation of offenders. This ambivalence of purpose must create appalling difficulties both for the courts and for the prison service, and it must be very confusing for offenders, many of whom could well be forgiven for failing to appreciate the difference between punishment and rehabilitation.

Perhaps this dilemma could be resolved by adopting a system whereby the court divides the sentence into two parts. The first part would be a relatively short period of punishment under humane but strict conditions, followed by a longer period of rehabilitation and training in a different establishment, and under completely different conditions. On the assumption that the major part of any sentence of more than a few months is intended for rehabilitation, the punishment part of the sentence might be limited to a maximum of ninety days – or for whatever maximum period is considered to be effective purely as punishment, as opposed to keeping dangerous criminals out of circulation. This part of the sentence would carry no possibility of remission, but the court might be able to order a further period of punishment for cases of particularly bad behaviour during the second part of the sentence. Such a system would also make it possible to allocate special establishments for those offenders who, it is considered, need to be kept out of circulation for the safety of society. The rehabilitation or second part of the sentence would consist of a basic period in a closed or open establishment, appropriate to the type of offender, reducible by remission or parole as at present, or by not more than one-third. As this part of the sentence would no longer be considered as punishment, it might also be made capable of extension in special cases in order to complete particular courses of education or training. Such a system might be particularly appropriate to young offenders who would be most likely to benefit from a rehabilitation programme containing a suitable mix of academic work, vocational or craft training, and a large dose of organised sport and physical recreation.

I believe that such a deliberately planned rehabilitation and training system would also help to integrate with the probation and resettlement phases in the process of returning offenders to normal life, in which the Associations for the Care and Resettlement of Offenders play such a vitally important part. Their work is genuinely humanitarian, but it should also be seen as a powerful method of preventing further crime.

However, there can be no absolute system for dealing with the prevention and detection of crime and the penalisation of offenders. There are obviously so many other imponderable factors: social background for instance – family, the community, housing conditions, the employer and particularly the school. Add to that lack of comprehension, mental handicap, the influence of drugs and alcohol, the sheer pressure of modern life, marital or job difficulties, racial discrimination. Then again, the powerful influence of conformity and convention. It can be almost impossible to resist the conventional standards of behaviour and activity of the group or community, and there are dozens of other considerations that make it extremely unwise to generalise.

I know something about boarding and Outward Bound schools, and I have visited a number of borstals and what used to be called approved schools, and it is quite evident to me that in broad principles they were all fairly similar. The difference of course is that boarding and Outward Bound schools are preventative, while the others are rehabilitative. The difference between boarding and non-boarding schools is not necessarily the standards of academic education, which seems to be the popular illusion, but the community life and the extra-curricular activities, such as sport, physical recreation, and cultural activities which are so much easier to organise in a boarding establishment.

This suggests to me that employers of young people, either as trainees or apprentices, could make a useful contribution to crime prevention by including a significant quota of sport and adventurous recreational training in the syllabus. It might even be an idea to allow young people to leave school at fifteen to complete their last compulsory year of education in carefully selected and approved programmes of training, which would have to include prescribed recreational and academic elements. The sort of things I have in mind are Armed Services schools for juniors, technical colleges and Industry Training Boards courses, and certain approved company apprentice schools. The challenges of these more adult activities, coupled with the exposure to challenging and exciting recreation of the type offered by Outward Bound schools, might possibly help to reduce the attraction of crime.

Social control also covers the difficult business of prevention. But there is one serious problem about any action intended to prevent things from happening. No one ever gets credit for preventing a crime. The same is true in the prevention of accidents. Who is to say that but for the preventive action, a crime or an accident would have happened? It is much easier to give credit to the medical team for saving a life after an accident, or to the rehabilitation and resettlement process after the crime has been committed.

Nevertheless the social control of crime begins with prevention. After that we need an efficient organisation for the detection of criminals, fair systems of trial and sentence, and a flexible organisation of measures to convert the offender to a law-abiding way of life through rehabilitation, training and resettlement. It will be an unending task, but I am quite convinced that we are capable of making a better job of it, particularly if we get down to a more practical understanding of human nature, and a more realistic appreciation of the pressures of modern society that lie at the cause of different kinds of criminal behaviour.

# 6
# Philosophy, Politics, Administration

# Philosophy, Politics, Administration

The broad-sounding title of this chapter was the title I chose for the 1979 Rede Lecture at Cambridge University. The lecture is reproduced here* in its original form, as I felt that neither theme nor presentation would be out of place in this short collection.

In February and March of 1979 I accompanied The Queen on a series of visits to most of the countries of the Arabian peninsula. Following that I went off on my own to Moscow in my capacity as President of the International Equestrian Federation to discuss preparations for the equestrian events at the Olympic Games in 1980. Then, changing my hat again, this time to that of President of the Central Council of Physical Recreation, I joined a delegation from that body to a series of meetings with the D.S.B., the German Sports Federation, before finally returning to London.

For anyone interested in systems and theories of government, the contrasts provided by this series of visits illustrated most vividly several of the underlying factors in the ideological warfare which seems to be bedevilling so much of present day international and community relations. The tour might well have been a practical course in the comparative study of government.

Society in the Arabian States is deeply influenced by

* *By courtesy of Cambridge University Press.*

Islam, which is a strict system focused on the belief and behaviour of the individual. The Sharia law deals with individual behaviour in great detail and even lays down rules about dress, primarily designed to ensure that there should be no ostentatious public display of wealth, particularly in the mosque, and to impress upon its followers their absolute equality in the eyes of the Almighty. Virtually nothing is said about how the temporal government should be organised. An Islamic State therefore merely means that the Koranic laws of belief and behaviour will be enforced. This, I believe, goes some way to explain why Islam can be the officially adopted philosophy in so many countries with very different forms of temporal government.

The system which exists in Arabia is therefore a combination of Islam with the social forms and customs evolved by a largely desert and nomadic people, and it was particularly interesting to see the way in which a governing system, developed for an entirely different life-style, was coping with the challenge of sudden massive wealth and industrialisation.

At first sight the system appears to be authoritarian, but this is an illusion enhanced by the Islamic teaching of respect for seniority, which is observed in a formal and social sense rather than as a reflection of power and influence. Conversely observance of the Islamic teaching of brotherhood and equality before God is less obvious, but plays a very important part in decision-making.

In practice dictatorship does not exist in the accepted sense in the Arabian countries, and indeed provided Arab custom is allied to Islamic precept it would be very difficult to achieve. The reason for this is an institution known as the 'Majlis', or sometimes 'Diwan'. The world 'majlis' is derived from the Arabic verb meaning 'to sit' so that it could be said to be a 'sitting'. The nearest equivalent in social and political terms might be the courts of medieval European monarchs. In the Arabian system anyone of any importance politically, socially or tribally is expected by custom to hold a majlis open to anyone who feels inclined to attend. Those with tribal responsibilities will be visited by anyone with something to discuss, usually in the evenings, while at the top end of a pyramid of such meetings is the majlis of senior government officials and ministers. The Ruler may spend as much as four to six hours a day in a series of sessions of his own majlis which every one of his subjects is entitled to attend, and to state his business or complaint.

A form of majlis also operates in the business world, and men of importance spend part of each day holding open house to their colleagues in their offices. The system also functions in reverse in that if the Ruler and his Government want to introduce some piece of legislation, the proposal is floated at the majlis, and will then find its way to discussion by every interested party before reactions, objections or approval find their way back to the Ruler. It may bear little relation to a formal parliamentary system, but there is no doubt that it provides very effectively for participation in decision-making.

The Gulf States have been trading and commercial communities for many years, and they have all been exposed to what we describe as Western culture, and several of them had in fact attempted a parliamentary system at various times, but owing to the pressures of vested interests, foreign embassies and international political groups the experiments were not exactly successful. Strangely enough the very men who were elected members of these assemblies, and whose behaviour in them brought about their collapse, seem to be working happily and effectively through the majlis system. However, this system has only been expected to work with a relatively small population. Whether it can remain effective under future conditions and particularly whether it can cope with a growing industrial population remains to be seen.

From Oman I flew to Moscow with a night stop in Istanbul and although my visit to Moscow was totally non-political in every sense of the word, it was naturally impossible not to be conscious of a quantum shift in the intellectual environment; but there was certainly no shift in the kindly and hospitable behaviour of my hosts of the Organising Committee for the Olympic Games.

The pervasive atmosphere of the Communist system, derived from Marxist philosophy, was as strong in Moscow as the Islamic influence was apparent in Arabia. It is almost impossible to put this atmosphere into words without appearing to have some political bias. Suffice it to say that under a system which suppresses a free market intentionally and free expression of necessity, and where the responsibility for planning and execution of any project from housing to manufacture is vested in a department of state, the consequences are fairly evident. Needless to say there is not much evidence to support Marx's prediction that 'the interference of the State power in social relations becomes superfluous in one sphere after another and then ceases of itself. . . . The State is not "abolished", it withers away.'*

I did not visit any museums in Moscow but I am pretty certain that the Soviet State, at least, is not in a 'museum of antiquities, by the side of the spinning wheel and the bronze axe,† where Engels expected it to be by now.

* *Socialism, Utopian and Scientific.*
† *Origins of the Family.*

Bakunin, the anarchist prophet, was rather nearer the mark when he said:

> The terms 'scientific socialist' and 'scientific socialism' . . . are sufficient to prove that the so-called 'people's State' will be nothing but a despotism over the masses, exercised by a new and quite small aristocracy of real or bogus scientists. The people . . . will be completely exempted from the task of governing and will be forced into the herd of the governed.

After two and a half days in the capital of what has now become an immense empire I flew on to Frankfurt in the German Federal Republic, a country with deep folk memories of the roaring inflation after the First World War and the traumatic experience of dictatorship and defeat under Hitler and his National Socialist German Workers' Party. Today it is probably the most materially successful of all the non-Communist European countries and considering the difficulties of achieving rational and consistent policies under a parliamentary and federal structure, there is every indication of a well-organised political and administrative system.

If you just read about theories of government and commentaries on economic issues, it is very easy to get the false impression that all men throughout the world are exactly alike in attitude, outlook and talent, and that all their problems have the same cause and can be solved in the same way. Indeed any suggestion that differences in character and aptitudes might exist is taken to mean that one or other of the many races of Homo Sapiens is superior to another. This completely distorts the picture, because superiority or inferiority is a matter of prejudice or opinion, while differences are matters of fact. This series of visits made it quite clear to me that while there are obvious differences in system and structure, there are equally obvious differences in character and outlook between the people of the countries I visited.

Yet whatever the differences in resources, geography, or national characteristics, all human communities large and small need some method, whether formal or informal, structured or flexible, for the purpose of managing their communal activities. While it is difficult to be objective and dangerous to generalise, I think it might be said that the difference between the systems can be measured by the amount of liberty that individuals are required to sacrifice for the sake of the system. Much as people value their liberty and independence, it seems to be generally acknowledged that some of this liberty has to be sacrificed in the interests of the community as a whole. The argument is about how much needs to be sacrificed and for what purpose. There is, of course, a significant difference between liberties given up voluntarily, that is by a process of democratic consensus, and those which are forcibly removed. As Thomas Jefferson said, 'I would rather be exposed to the inconveniences attending too much liberty than those attending too small a degree of it.'

Supporters of the democratic principle naturally believe that theirs is the only system capable of achieving a consensus. However a formal representative system cannot guarantee that a community will be governed by consensus any more than efficient administration can be guaranteed by the sheer size of a bureaucracy. Furthermore both the political decision-making system and the administrative structure are deeply influenced in one way or another by the religious, philosophical or economic concepts, generally accepted by the majority or enforced by the most powerful group within the community.

Therefore any system of government comprises, in very broad terms, these three factors: first, a common purpose or a generally accepted religious or political philosophy; second, a system of policy-making; and third, an executive or administrative structure capable of implementing policy decisions. I want to discuss the relationship of these three factors to each other and their influence on the community as a whole.

The evidence of history seems to suggest that when these three factors, which for simplicity rather than absolute accuracy I would like to describe as philosophy, politics and administration – when these three are in balance the general way of life appears to be more tolerant and capable of greater social and material progress. If by chance the system gets out of balance and any one of the factors comes to acquire a dominating influence or a position of exceptional power, the system becomes intolerant and inflexible and both the institutions within the State and particularly the individual citizen are made to suffer. For example, the more powerful and aggressive the philosophy the fewer options are open to politicians, institutions and individuals. Alternatively, if the political factor takes the shape of a one-party State or a parliament dominated for many years by one party, the code of morality and ethics normally supplied by the religious philosophy is liable to be ignored and once again it is the individual who suffers, as political ends are made to justify administrative means.

Whether the element of philosophy is deliberately suppressed or removed by changing fashion, or in the case of Hitler's government where the philosophy of Nietzsche was used to justify rather than to inspire its activities, the consequences are much the same. The politicians and administrators are left to organise things to suit themselves.

Historically battles have been between over-powerful executives or theocracies challenged by democratic political parties. It can happen, but it is less common for the professional administrators on their own to achieve such a position of power and influence within the State that it becomes almost impossible for them to be challenged by political parties or influenced by the philosophy. Eventually such an executive or bureaucracy is liable to degenerate into a vested interest and it either becomes corrupt, inflexibly and inefficiently bureaucratic, or simply tyrannical.

I cannot resist the temptation to parody a paragraph by Marx on money power by substituting status in the bureaucratic hierarchy. It would go like this:

> My power is as great as the power of my status. The attributes and essential strength of status are those of myself, its owner. It is not my own personality which decides what I am and what I can do. I may be ugly, but I can coerce the prettiest woman alive; consequently I am not ugly, since status destroys the repellent power of ugliness. I may be lame, but my status entitles me to a car, therefore I am not lame. I may be bad, dishonest, ruthless and narrow-minded but status ensures respect for itself and its possessor. Status is the supreme good, and a man who has it must be good also.

Thomas Jefferson put it more shortly: 'Whenever a man has cast a longing eye on offices, a rottenness begins in his conduct.'

The danger of any system in which the three factors are not in balance is that any limits to interference in the legitimate activities of private citizens and institutions have to be self-imposed by some conscious recognition of the needs of individuals and what are deemed to be their rights. Such limits can only be conceived by people who are convinced of the primary importance of the liberty of individuals and are prepared to accept that each one is entitled to his own point of view, and his own freedom of action and expression within an objective law. The ambition for, or the acquisition of, dominant power by any one factor is obviously incompatible with this concept.

In the ordinary course of events the eventual popular reaction to an unbalanced acquisition of power is a more or less violent revolution. Such revolutions, in most cases against over-powerful executives, have taken place in almost all the major nations of the Northern Hemisphere as well as elsewhere. The first was in Britain in 1642, followed by the U.S.A. in 1777, France in 1789, the U.S.S.R. in 1917 and Germany in 1918. In each case the eventual outcome was a completely reorganised general system of government.

In Britain the system evolved into a parliamentary democracy. It is perhaps worth noting that it was originally based on three Estates, the Lords Spiritual and Temporal, and Commons, under a constitutional monarchy. For my purposes the Lords Temporal and Commons constitute the single political estate, but the point is that the inclusion of the Church suggests that the value of a philosophy as a counterbalance to purely pragmatic political ambition or absolute executive power has been very well understood in this country for many years. It could be argued that with the relative decline in the influence of the Lords Spiritual, the balance of our system has been disturbed.

The U.S. Constitution emerged from a War of Independence, rather than from an internal social revolution followed by a dictatorship as in the other cases. The Founding Fathers were liberals and democrats, and many were devout

Christians, and they were living in what was still a pioneering community without an entrenched ecclesiastical or military establishment or the deeply ingrained social structures of the old world. They were able, therefore, to take full advantage of this unique opportunity to start all over again. In the end they created a system based firmly on Christian philosophy, a democratic political structure and a controlled administration which has stood both the test of time, a civil and two world wars and an astonishing rate of economic growth, without demanding more than a bare minimum of the sacrifice of personal liberty.

This system is now so deeply entrenched that the only apparent aspect is the jockeying for political power between two groups of professional opponents, both of which are equally intent on controlling the executive and the administration through the system of checks and balances incorporated in the Constitution. After several false starts Germany has finally adopted a similar system, and let us hope that it proves as successful and enduring as that of the U.S.A. The French seem to have experienced the longest period of post-revolutionary instability, but thanks to the Napoleonic influence on the administrative structure and the reorganisation of the Constitution in the 1960s she is at last enjoying a period of considerable success and stability. With these three examples it is rather tempting to speculate whether the U.S.S.R. is going to repeat the pattern of revolution and dictatorship, leading eventually to a more liberal and tolerant system.

In primitive societies the purpose or the objective of the community was dictated by circumstances, and in most cases was simply the need to survive under the conditions prevailing. It might involve nothing more complicated than the choice of a leader to organise a hunting party or defence against attack. The circumstances may change, such as the transition from an agrarian to an industrialised society, and the purpose may become more complicated or ambitious, such as the establishment of a system based on an intellectual theory, as in Communism, but the need for a process of decision-making and the need for some sort of organisation to manage cooperative activity remains the same.

Naturally these also have to evolve and adapt to changing demands and circumstances. I need hardly add that those groups or nations who manage to organise themselves most effectively, whether they are endowed with natural resources or not, are the most likely to be productive, peaceful and prosperous. A wealth of natural resources may allow more mistakes and inefficiency, but they certainly do not guarantee a fair political system or an efficient administration. Neither is there any convincing evidence that even the most ambitious political philosophy or any divinely inspired religious doctrine can, of themselves, prevent an administration becoming a lumbering and oppressive bureaucracy.

To oversimplify rather drastically: where politicians are concerned about what ought to be done and administrators are concerned with what can be done, it seems to me that philosophers are concerned with ideologies, explanations of history, and theories to account for human thoughts and actions and the conclusions derived from them. In other words, the purpose for doing something. Philosophy therefore establishes, either directly or by implication, the ground rules for the game of life. Those who understand the arguments, and are convinced that the conclusions are good ones, or at least that they are conveniently desirable from their own point of view, then set about devising an interpretation of these conclusions in terms of their practical application to organised human life.

It is as if the philosophers had concluded that playing games appeared to allow the best chance for mankind to fulfil itself, or to redeem itself, or for whatever reason happens to strike them at the time. Those who are convinced by these ideas, who, for simplicity, might be described as the politicians, then have a debate about whether the people are most likely to be uplifted by sports of their own choice or whether, say, a team-type game like football, or an individual-type game like golf would be more appropriate. Meanwhile the people would probably much rather enjoy drinking, smoking and watching television; but no matter, the proper interpretation of the philosophy demands that golf should be played.

The politicians having decided on the rules of the chosen game, the administrator is employed to get on and arrange it. Whereupon he designs the courses, and provides the officials in the form of judges, umpires and referees to see that the rules are complied with. He arranges for coaches, matches and championships, and all the other tiresome details that finally make it possible for the individual to benefit, or otherwise, from the wisdom of the philosopher.

Unfortunately, human nature being what it is, it does not take long for the more competitive or enterprising players to discover loopholes in the rules, or for officials to lose their impartiality.

So once again the politicians are required to amend the rules and to keep a stricter eye on the officials. Experience in the control and administration of sports and games is that, in the interest of fairness and impartiality, the people who write the rules and those who act as officials are not permitted to take part in the game at the same time. The same unfortunately cannot be said for some forms of government. In some systems the whole game – apart from a few caddies –

has been taken over by the State. In other systems, the term 'mixed economy' means that the ordinary players find that both politicians and administrators are taking part both as players as well as referees. Meanwhile the philosopher, whose whole idea it was, is inclined to be forgotten.

History seems to suggest that this sort of relationship – between philosophy, politics and administration – is present in all the ancient, and indeed in all the modern, civilisations. However, history is also full of examples of good intentions going wrong. I rather doubt whether the early Marxists ever imagined that their doctrine would lead to Stalin's tyranny over the Soviet Union. And just listen to what Marx had to say about censorship of the press:

> A censored press is a thing without a backbone, a vampire of slavery, a civilised monstrosity, a scented freak of nature. Is there any further need to prove that freedom is in accordance with the essence of the press, and that censorship is contrary to it?*

But then to be fair I suppose you could say that the Inquisition was bad luck on St. Paul.

The fact is that the success of a tolerant, liberal system depends to a large extent on a general acceptance of standards of human behaviour which recognise the need for social discipline by everyone within an ordered framework, but which are based on a philosophy of personal responsibility. But it is exactly this general acceptance by voluntary means which is so difficult to achieve.

In any homogeneous organisation or institution with one single and obvious purpose the problem is not too difficult. In essence it comprises two parts, the selection of leaders or

* *Deutsche Jahrbücher.*

policy- and decision-makers, and the development of an administrative structure designed to execute policy decisions. In practice it usually happens that both the policy-makers and the administrators are practising members of the organisation itself who are selected by one process or another to undertake the 'political' management of the affairs of their organisation as an extra chore.

The major Christian churches and universities are good examples of this type of internal self-management carried on simultaneously with their primary operational purposes. Universities are of course particularly fortunate as they are unique among all institutions in that they are controlled entirely by students and ex-students. This system of internal self-government is a simple and genuine form of democracy and it is the usual method of managing every kind of institution in this country, from Trinity House to the Stock Exchange; but with the notable exception of such relatively recent institutions which have come to be known as 'Quangos' or Quasi-Autonomous Government Organisations, whose members are appointed by patronage and from which the element of representative self-government and accountability has been virtually excluded.

The self-government of institutions is a vital element in any society which aspires to be democratic, and furthermore it has the great advantage in that it allows governments to concentrate on the business for which only governments can be responsible.

While it is perfectly true that a bad management structure can inhibit the establishment of harmonious human relations, and consequently prevent sensible decisions being taken, even the very best management structure cannot hope to work without the will to make it work, and human nature being what it is, the will to make a system work is always stronger where the interests of individuals are coincident or at least compatible with the interests of the system as a whole.

As Marx put it: 'The purpose of the true state is not that each citizen should devote himself to the general cause as though to a particular one, but that the general cause should be truly general, i.e. the cause of every citizen.'*

This precept applies to every system of government, where even the most rational and realistic political structures can be rendered utterly meaningless if ambitious and unscrupulous politicians and administrators are tempted to exploit the system in their interest, rather than to make it work for the purpose for which it was intended. It also applies, in a rather different sense, to organisations intended to produce goods or services. These cannot function successfully unless there is a sensible structure, an accepted standard of behaviour, and a general will to cooperate within that structure to achieve the objective, and as this cooperation needs to take place between people of all kinds of talents and qualities, the will to cooperate is absolutely vital.

Philosophers and political scientists over the ages have concerned themselves, amongst other things, with such imponderables as justice, equity, morality, and the rights and responsibilities of the individual and the purpose of governments. There have been many different schools of thought, some emphasising one aspect and some another, but in the end it seems to be possible to divide them into two broad camps.

Again to oversimplify, one camp concentrates on reason and logic; it talks about 'mankind' and 'humanity', and generalises man into a sort of universal substance. To take the

* *Critique of Hegel's Philosophy of Right.*

analogy with golf a stage further, it might be said that the utopia of the 'mankind' camp is a situation where a benevolent state arranges for everyone to score a hole in one at each attempt regardless of cost. The other camp concentrates on the individual and on his total nature, and believes that the whole value of the game is the constant striving for perfection, and the personal satisfaction to be gained by individual improvement.

This division of attitude among philosophers has been developing over many centuries. It might be argued that one stream of thought has come down through Plato, and, in the main, through European thinkers culminating in the Hegelians and Marx. It seems to have started out with a supposition that human existence on earth could achieve an ideal state simply by the operation of reasoned thought, and that once all men came to recognise the advantages of a system created by pure reason they would naturally and obviously accept the situation, although it is not always clear exactly who is to decide what is reasonable and rational for everyone beyond any dispute.

In this argument mankind as a whole is treated as if it were some sort of sentient being with a life-span covering the whole of human existence. Consequently mankind is thought capable of reacting as a whole and gradually growing in wisdom, understanding and brotherly love with an idealised State as the instrument for achieving this ideal situation. This stream of thought has inclined to the view that it is only the State, inspired by reason and rational intelligence, that can decide what is good for its people, and what and how they should do and think.

I suspect that it is this generalisation of man, this abstract concept of humanity, this segregation of the reasoning mind from the complex of emotions and intuitions which has led to so many generalised economic theories, which treat individuals only as units for statistics and parts of averages. In turn this statistical approach encourages the idea that people can be tucked away in neat categories of such things as income group, technical or professional qualifications or class, and that once in a category for one purpose they are in the same category for all purposes.

One of the consequences of generalisation is that issues become confused. For instance it makes it possible to equate group or national independence with the liberty of the individual. In practice these are very different indeed, as I suspect the people of several of the more recently independent countries have discovered to their cost. Furthermore it suggests certain groups are automatically composed of undesirable and anti-social characters while others are inevitably full of a most saint-like creatures. Even a very limited experience of human nature reveals the fallacy of any such idea.

Generalisation of this sort is enjoying a great vogue in this country at the moment. There is much talk of wealth creation and distribution, the importance of engineering and manufacturing, and such abstract concepts as labour and management, and that most nebulous of all generalisations, the national economy. All these things are nothing more than convenient labels, they are sums, percentages or averages of individual activity, but you cannot change the activity of individuals simply by demanding changes to the sum of their activities. For instance engineering does not create the engineer; engineering is created by people with particular talents and ambitions.

That is not to say that individuals cannot act corporately. In some cases the individual can avoid responsibility by pleading loyalty to a group. On the other hand membership of a group with a strong sense of service can induce a higher standard of behaviour in an individual than he could achieve on his own.

Perhaps the most significant development in the 'mankind' stream of philosophy was inspired, if not directly enunciated, by Hegel. In effect philosophy was no longer to be considered simply as an attempt to interpret human history, or to influence human behaviour, but as a deliberate endeavour to influence the future of mankind as a whole by transforming what are believed to be rational concepts into practical structures. As Marx put it in a frequently quoted passage: 'The philosophers have only interpreted the world in various ways, the point however is to change it!' It is this direct and dominant association of an aggressive philosophy with politics and administration which distinguishes the Marxist-Socialist type of government systems which are derived from it.

The other stream of philosophy seems to come down through the Old Testament prophets and perhaps the Sophists, and then through Christ and Mohammed, as far as Europe and the Middle East are concerned, and through the Buddha further east. The general concept of this stream seems to be that in the normal course of events the world is at best a neutral, if not an actively wicked place, which can only be made tolerable by the commitment of individuals to what is good and right. It holds that it is not the structures and organisations of states or groups which dictate the fate of nations, but the cumulative effect of its individual members each acting during his limited life-span under the compulsion of a religious and moral code of practice. In this stream there is every latitude for the individual to exercise responsibility in whatever legitimate way he may choose, always provided he shows concern for the unfortunate, and consideration to all men.

However, the individual orientated systems are dependent for their success on the voluntary acceptance, by at least a large majority, of certain standards of human behaviour and relationship to one another. As these standards have to be inculcated into every child of every succeeding generation it is obviously impossible to maintain these standards at a uniformly high level at all times, and in all sections of the community.

Furthermore there will always be a proportion of the population which inevitably loses out in the competitive scramble for material survival, and whose situation is made to look even worse by those who have been particularly successful. Then there are those who simply do not wish to conform to the accepted philosophy and these have certainly been cruelly persecuted from time to time, but both the disadvantage and the intolerance have always been contrary to the basic precepts of this stream of philosophy.

In the Plato-Marxist stream, on the other hand, there is no room for those who disagree with the system, or who cannot bring themselves to believe that the State is anything other than a bunch of fallible and ambitious mortals whose sole justification for their monopoly of power is that they claim to know better than their fellow citizens, and are prepared to use any means to enforce conformity. In exchange for conforming the claim is made, though not always substantiated in practice, that no one need suffer from sheer material misfortune.

It is easy enough to show that in purely statistical terms the bulk of the populations living under either system enjoy largely comparable material standards. The real differences only become apparent when you compare the state of the disadvantaged, in the first case due to such things as unemployment, and various forms of material deprivation as against police harassment, concentration camps and the loss of freedom of speech and of enterprise; sins of omission against sins of commission.

As might have been expected, the politically orientated philosophies maintain that class, religion, private property and the division of labour are the causes of all mankind's troubles, while the moral or religious philosophies claim that the love of money is the root of all evil. In consequence, the former advocate economic solutions and material egalitarianism while the latter are concerned with spiritual egalitarianism or equality before God and the law, and the salvation of the individual soul through charity, humility and self-control.

It is perhaps symptomatic that the former is accused of denying human rights while the latter is accused of denying social justice. The former believes in revolution and conversion by violence while the latter hopes to achieve a spiritual revolution in the minds of individuals, and it is worth remembering that more people have renounced violence, wealth and material comfort for the sake of their God than they have for the sake of their political party.

The trouble seems to be that the solutions put forward by the materialist philosophers and economic theorists have caused as many problems as they claim to have solved. Indeed in many cases decisions dictated by theory and subjective assessment have been shown in practice to have exactly the opposite effect to that intended. It is quite possible that the conditions in manufacturing industry 150 years ago caused alienation and dehumanisation. The danger today appears to be that the sheer volume of legislation and the inflexibility of bureaucratic structures are creating a similar sense of alienation and the dehumanisation of individuals by the all-powerful and impersonal State.

It may well be that the whole discussion about participation and the wish to be involved in decision-making at work has stemmed from the erosion of the ability of individuals to participate in their domestic decision-making as citizens and parents.

One major factor which all the politically and economically orientated philosophers have had to contend with, and which many of them have used as a criticism of their opponents, is that views and analyses are inevitably influenced by personal experience and particularly by the social and economic conditions prevailing at the time they were formulated. In other words there has always been the danger that circumstances might change and so render their ideas and remedies irrelevant.

In philosophies dealing with human nature and personal behaviour, on the other hand, the central subject has not changed in any marked degree during recorded history and is no more likely to do so in the future.

On the whole it seems that the weakness of the materialist system comes from a disregard for the spirit of men, while that in the spiritual system is claimed to be an apparent inability to provide for the material needs of the poor and handicapped. While it looks as if the former can only be cured by a considerable shift in the State philosophy, no system has been able to do more than to alleviate the latter, and then only by a combination of administrative measures, public funds and voluntary service.

Yet in general terms there really is no great argument about intentions. Both systems are equally committed in principle to the welfare of all mankind, and both find their particular groups of disadvantaged a considerable embarrassment. Both are deeply concerned to remove the disadvantages, in the one case by finding means of relieving poverty and handicap, and in the other by all sorts of attempts to convert intellectual opposition into conformity and support. Both agree about the desirability of a so-called democratic system, but as they interpret the meaning of the word in different senses they disagree fundamentally on the structure of the government system, and the consequent relationship between the State and the people or the State and the individual.

In one respect at least things could be easier for future generations in that, given that they have any choice at all in the matter, they will be able to compare systems of government derived from both streams of philosophy in practical operation. Thcy will in all probability ignore it, but the evidence will be there for all to see that the one system has not been able to deliver the promised utopia in the present world, while the other may not be able to prove that everlasting bliss will be achieved in the world to come, but at least it puts the blame for present ills where it belongs, on people and not on structures.

Whatever their technical and scientific achievements, I suspect that the problems of managing and governing men will continue to plague every generation, but my guess is that finding workable solutions to these problems has not been made any easier by those philosophers who have claimed to have found the one all-embracing solution to the problems of the whole of mankind. Paradoxically the materialist line of reasoning has contributed a great deal to our understanding of the development of some human communities and civilisations, but there is little evidence to suggest that the lot of men has been greatly improved either spiritually or materially by the implementation of the theories of the materialist philosophers. Their erudition and cleverness is not in doubt, but it would seem that their understanding of the practical facts of human existence was perhaps rather more limited and their faith in the nobler aspects of human nature almost non-existent.

Equally there is no doubt about their good intentions, but somehow or other their over-simplification of the issues seems to have stimulated an unwarranted confidence in the effectiveness of the political and administrative systems which are derived from their ideas. This self-righteous paternalism has in turn created a bitter political confrontation and alienation between government bureaucracies and the private citizen.

It was clearly never intended to create such arbitrary and damaging divisions in human society, and now that experience seems to suggest that they hold out little promise of achieving greater social harmony and cooperation, perhaps it is time for a new initiative in the development of political philosophies.

In the 150 years since Marx developed his ideas, the world has experienced a series of industrial, social and scientific explosions which have created the modern urban-industrial civilisations within wholly new material and intellectual environments and with a wholly new dimension in living standards. Many of the old problems still remain, but these new circumstances would appear to demand a new analysis and a new set of directions for the future, taking into account the present levels of public education and reflecting a better appreciation of the state of medical and scientific knowledge in the latter part of the twentieth century. It is now 200 years since the Industrial Revolution, and practices in industrial and commercial enterprises have come a very long way in that time and any new thinking should be firmly based on a realistic assessment of the best and most successful of them. But above all we must never again allow any system to ignore both the best or the worst in human nature.

There is every reason to believe that human nature will remain much as it always has been, which means that such classic problems as selfishness and dishonesty, cheating and exploitation, crime and punishment, unscrupulous ambition and corruption in public administration are likely to continue to provide headaches for every community for as long as this planet is able to support its load of humanity. But these more sordid features need to be balanced against the genuine kindliness and concern, the generosity and self-denial which is to be found in so many more people in all walks of life, and particularly against the limitless capacity of people to respond to the inspiration of religious and moral teaching.

Of one thing I am absolutely convinced. There cannot be any satisfactory future for the so-called silent majority if the elements of philosophy, politics and administration remain out of balance and continue to create conflict and confrontation between governments and people.

# 7
# Satisfaction and Contentment

# Satisfaction and Contentment

This piece was part of my speech at the opening of the 1980 Commonwealth Study Conference in Canada* and I suppose I was merely expanding on Shakespeare's comment when he made Caesar say:

> Why, man, he doth bestride the narrow world
> Like a Colossus; and we petty men
> Walk under his huge legs, and peep about
> To find ourselves dishonourable graves.
> Men at some time are masters of their fates;
> The fault, dear Brutus, is not in our stars,
> But in ourselves . . .

The purpose of this series of Commonwealth Study Conferences is to allow the decision-makers of tomorrow to take their noses off the grindstone and to stand back long enough to get a general view of human life in the modern urban/industrial complex.

The contemporary urban/industrial complex, based on the discoveries of science and the products of technology, is an entirely new experience for humanity. It took hundreds of generations for Homo Sapiens, the hunter, to adapt to the life-style of Homo Sapiens, the cultivator. So far there have only been perhaps five or six generations since the Industrial Revolution ushered in mechanised factories and mass

* Queen's University, Kingston, Ontario, 19 May 1980.

production techniques, the large-scale exploitation of non-renewable resources and the concentration of the population in huge cities.

Industrialisation has also produced other problems. Agriculture may have been affected by developing technology, but provided it does not over-exploit them, it can at least rely on renewable raw materials and on the fact that people will always need food. The industrial production of consumer and capital goods, on the other hand, is subject to massive fluctuations. A mine is worked out, and a whole community loses its purpose and livelihood; a product is no longer required and a whole factory has to close down; a new technology appears, such as micro-processors, and the work and employment patterns of whole industries have to be reorganised virtually overnight. Equally important is the fact that the industrial worker is wholly dependent on some person or organisation providing him with an opportunity to work for his living. Unlike the rural worker, he cannot fall back on a smallholding or casual seasonal labour. There is no doubt about the great advantages of industrial work, when you have got it, but the disadvantages are far greater if you cannot get it.

There is also a good deal of evidence that exposure to the natural world and all its uncertainties provides an important element in the education for children for life. This element is lacking in the wholly mechanical environment of the big industrial cities. But these are only some of the direct problems created by industrialisation – the indirect problems are just as daunting. After thousands of years of relative immobility, people have suddenly been offered opportunities for personal transport that are rapidly changing the social pattern of our cities. At one time, people belonged to the same community for living, working, recreation and worship;

today it is possible to do each of these things in completely separate communities. The ability of the more affluent to live outside the city and commute to work has led to the departure of the natural social leaders in the city communities and this may well have contributed to the decay of inner cities.

Modern medicine and food production has reduced infant mortality and allowed more people to stay alive and grow to old age. The consequent population explosion is itself partly the cause of employment problems as well as the rapidly increasing drain on natural and mineral resources.

Perhaps the most worrying consequence of industrial technology is the fear and anxiety caused by the development of such advanced and only partially understood techniques as nuclear power, and also of sophisticated and powerful military weapons and equipment, particularly when it gets into the hands of criminals and terrorists. All in all, it is really not altogether surprising that poor old Homo Sapiens is finding it rather difficult to adapt from cultivation and rural life to factory work and city life.

Taken individually, I think it would be true to say that each of the technological developments of the industrial age has made a positive contribution to human convenience, but taken together, and with all their secondary effects, they have created an immense challenge to human adaptability.

That the process is not going altogether smoothly seems to be demonstrated by the exceptional amount of social conflict which is affecting the large urban/industrial complexes all over the world. While it takes some exceptional event to cause social disturbance in rural communities, riots, vandalism, protest marches, political extremism and crime all appear to be the natural state of affairs in many cities. It is therefore only reasonable to conclude from this that the average man is not entirely compatible with, or has not yet adapted to, the sort of life-style industrialisation and urbanisation has created for him. To make matters worse, it is now beginning to look as if human communities are going to have to face yet another major shift in life-style. The threatened exhaustion of fossil fuels and non-renewable resources, upon which the whole industrial system depends, spells out a very clear message. Our Planet Earth will not be able to sustain the present world population, at even its present standards, for very much longer, and if the population continues to increase at the present rate, standards will inevitably have to fall, unpleasantly for the richer and catastrophically for the poorer communities.

In recent years we have all tended to assume that the world's problems can be solved by national governments and international organisations with the help of scientists and engineers, and a book of ideological instructions. I think it is becoming more and more apparent that the future direction of events depends as much upon the commonsense micro-decisions of millions of properly educated people in positions of limited authority, as it does on the anonymous macro-decisions of governments and international agencies. Indeed, when it comes to controlling the size of the human population, the decisions rest exclusively with actual and potential parents.

It is, of course, easy enough to list all the practical problems facing today's decision-makers, but they are really the least of our difficulties. Much more important are the problems we create for ourselves. By that I mean faulty theories, biased analyses, prejudiced attitudes, the subversion of rational arguments by irrational emotions; in fact, by the operation of the ordinary factors of human nature, factors which have always been part of the human make-up.

Every nation in the world is composed of racial, linguistic, cultural or religious groups or minorities, but these are not created by industrialisation or by science or by technology. The problems they produce are products of the human spirit and the personality of individuals. Castes and classes are not the products of ideologies any more than individual intelligence and enterprise are the products of an educational system. The former are creations of human nature and the latter derive from a mixture of chance and genetics.

It may not be easy to overcome the weaknesses in our human nature, but that is no reason why we should not make an attempt to recognise and understand them. At least the ancients were sufficiently aware of them to list the Seven Deadly Sins and to accept the need for the Ten Commandments, even if they did not always abide by them. Until each of us accepts that our problems are not created by such abstract concepts as industry, religion, capitalism, the Third World, the bourgeoisie or the world economy, but by our own individual standards of morality, behaviour and competence, we shall never begin to cope with the causes of our discontents.

There is a very big difference between being intelligent and being capable or being compassionate; and, equally, there is absolutely no correlation between intelligence, capability and stupidity, on the one hand, with goodness and badness, and neither is there any necessary relationship between prosperity and civilised behaviour or, for that matter, between knowledge and wisdom. Academic brilliance is not automatically linked with high moral standards and that splendid phrase 'high moral standards' is only another way of saying 'self-control'.

Just imagine uncontrolled human nature on the loose, indulging in every instinct and passing fancy without thought for the consequences, every action dictated by a selfish view of what seems expedient at the moment. Even animal communities cannot survive under those conditions.

No society can be called civilised if it consists of brilliant crooks, ambitious but incompetent intellectuals, militant extremists and selfish rich, though of course you cannot get rid of them altogether; but experience has shown that it is better to encourage honesty and competence, tolerance and charity. Life may have become a great deal more complicated since the industrial and scientific revolutions, and such occupations as industry and commerce and administration and medicine and even sport may have assumed greater significance in the economic and social fabric of the state; but in the end civilised standards still depend absolutely on the way people treat each other as people. The clue to a relaxed, liberal and free society is the behaviour of its individual members, whatever their occupation, whatever their level of intelligence, and whatever their capability, and it is no excuse to use membership of a group such as management, or a trade union or the Civil Service or a political party to escape from the responsibility of personal civilised standards and behaviour at all times, both in public and in private.

In the final analysis only individuals can feel satisfaction and contentment and, as the evidence of history shows, these cannot be guaranteed by some patent ideology or political system, or even by material prosperity alone. In the end satisfaction and contentment are created by the relationships between one individual and another at work, in the community and in the home.

You do not have to be a practising Christian to see that human rights begin with Christ's teaching—'Always treat others as you would like them to treat you.'